CARÊME

Praise for *Carême*

'A magnificent work. Ian Kelly is at the vanguard of the new rock'n'roll of culinary literature' Anthony Bourdain

'A glistening pudding in its own right ... Makes for brilliant reading and, if you have a spirit of adventure, brilliant cooking too. For this is as much a recipe book as a history' Giles Coren, *The Times*

'The recipes are fascinating to read, mostly because they make you marvel at what Carême was able to do with only the most rudimentary tools, with nary a blender to stand naked behind' *Los Angeles Times*

'Kelly feasts on the wealth of source material; his fine book offers a recipe at the end of each chapter, plus more in an appendix' *Publisher's Weekly*

'Cuisinier, architect and one of the most prolific writers of the nineteenth century, Carême was the founder of a classic cuisine that would influence generations of chefs. In this well-researched book, Ian Kelly deftly recounts the exploits of this remarkable man' Jacques Pépin

'Dazzling, theatrical, peppered with detail and served up with humour, style and a close understanding of the workings of kitchens then and now, *Carême* is a unique experience of food as drama and as part of our history' Julian Fellowes, writer and executive producer of *Downton Abbey*

'Carême invented a new way of cooking and Kelly cooked up a new way of writing about food. Wild, delicious and rarefied. A classic' Damian Barr

'Ian Kelly's valuable and pleasurable addition to the literature of food combines an eye for the richness of historic detail with a solid sense of culinary crafts. While stimulating our palates, it breathes a life into a critical period in the building of modern Europe' Mark Kurlansky

'Antonin Carême, the chef of chefs, was a legend in his own time and as artful a publicist as any of today's celebrity cooks. His story is a natural for an epic tale and Ian Kelly brings Carême's restless spirit back to life along with a tableau of *la grande cuisine* two hundred years ago' Anne Willan, founder of the École de Cuisine La Varenne

'Ian Kelly has done a wonderful job, not only of depicting Carême's culinary genius beautifully but of introducing us to his extraordinary personal life as well. I enjoyed reading this book immensely and recommend it to culinary historians and food buffs everywhere' Daniel Boulud, founder of Café Boulud

CARÊME

The First Celebrity Chef

IAN KELLY

B L O O M S B U R Y

LONDON · OXFORD · NEW YORK · NEW DELHI · SYDNEY

BLOOMSBURY PUBLISHING
Bloomsbury Publishing Plc
50 Bedford Square, London, WC1B 3DP, UK
Bloomsbury Publishing Ireland Limited,
29 Earlsfort Terrace, Dublin 2, D02 AY28, Ireland

BLOOMSBURY, BLOOMSBURY PUBLISHING and the Diana logo
are trademarks of Bloomsbury Publishing Plc

First published in Great Britain as *Cooking for Kings* by Short Books in 2003
This paperback edition published 2025

A catalogue record for this book is available from the British Library

ISBN: PB: 978-1-5266-8977-1; eBook: 978-1-5266-9370-9;
ePDF: 978-1-5266-9369-3

2 4 6 8 10 9 7 5 3 1

Typeset by Ed Pickford

Printed and bound in Great Britain by Clays Ltd, Elcograf S.p.A.

To find out more about our authors and books visit
www.bloomsbury.com and sign up for our newsletters

For product-safety-related questions contact productsafety@bloomsbury.com

For Mum and Dad

Contents

Prologue

You have what it takes to succeed, little one,
go forth and do so.

Jean Gilbert Carême to his nine-year-old son, Antonin, 1792

I write this at the family kitchen table, while cooking Thanksgiving dinner. It will be my father's last Thanksgiving, he tells me, not with drama or sadness, just with the resignation of a retired pathologist in the face of ineluctable results and a habit of good timekeeping. My dad. My mother manoeuvres around her kitchen on a walking-frame, no easy task as commis-chef, brandishing in arthritic hands the cooking implements I remember from my childhood, many of them American, the ones with which she taught me to cook from a scrapbook of recipes here by my side.

I wrote *Carême* twenty-one years ago. I know this as my son was born that year and the midwives all had pâtisserie from the confectioner's where I had trained, a keen young historian then, to understand Carême's pastry-craft. My son and I recently created a menu together for his 21st birthday.

The journey from page to stage to screen has taken that long. Though now, when I look back, this story and this lifetime's adventure in books and drama with Antonin Carême is measured out, as lives should be, by meals.

My parents had a love of Thanksgiving from their time as young marrieds in Philadelphia. Pumpkin and turkey, allspice and regrets. Gratitude, too. Thanksgiving has a particular smell; not quite Christmas, autumnal and, once-upon-a-time in both my family as in politics, uncomplicated. No longer. I think my earliest taste-memory was the tongue-lash of cranberry, and for that matter, the soft yielding of yams and grilled pink marshmallows. It was the 1970s. My mother's Thanksgivings in time became inflected instead with British and indeed French styles – potatoes Dauphinoise, bread sauce – and with personal touches and memories, as family feasts do. She preferred Christmas. The thing about food of course is that you cannot be around it without memories. If you are lucky, as I have been, these are memories of family and of love. Carême's story, suffused with the tastes and smells of a lost era was inflected in turn with family loss and love. It was also gilded with glamour and with royalty, beset with violence and vaulting ambition, stage-set against epic historical panoramas in an age of revolution and at the dawn of modernity. It was quite a story. As it happened, Carême's drama came into my life as I was about to become a father myself, cooking late-night curries in the hope of harrying an unwilling baby into the world. Carême has been with me ever since, along with my children, and for all their short lives, one 'before I die' over-vaulting ambition for me was always to bring Carême to the screen. Because this story – his story – that I happened upon by accident, obsessed upon for two decades, while my children grew and other books and plays and projects came and went, this story that became the stuff of biography and then of documentary, of stage play and even daytime television, was always and also and ultimately for me the stuff of screen drama. That was why I wrote it. And here we are.

CHAPTER 1

A Feast for Epicures

The recipe that I am going to sketch for you here is quick and simple: my life has not gone quite as planned.

Antonin Carême, *Souvenirs inédits*

Paris, 6 July 1829. Early evening. A hired barouche rattles up the Champs-Elysées. Inside: a noblewoman so tiny her close-cropped wig is barely visible through the carriage's open window. Lady Morgan, travel writer, Irish radical and wit, is reflecting upon her dinner invitation, and upon food.

'You are going to dine at the first table in France – in Europe!' she had been told. 'You are going to judge, and taste for yourself, the genius!'

An invitation from the Rothschilds had incited both jealousy and awe at Lady Morgan's Paris lodgings, and not just because James and Betty de Rothschild were the richest couple in France. Their chef, known to everyone, was Antonin Carême. And all Paris, including Lady Morgan, wanted to eat *à la Carême*. She already knew all about him: the wedding cake he had cooked for Napoleon and his empress, the gargantuan banquets he had cooked for the Tsar of Russia, the elaborate pâtés he had created for the Prince Regent in London (which she remembered being sold illicitly from the palace kitchens at exorbitant prices). She had even read Carême's books.

Perhaps Lady Morgan had skipped over the thousands of recipes, but she had read, wide-eyed, his descriptions of life 'below stairs' in St Petersburg, Paris and the Brighton Pavilion, and she knew the rags-to-riches tale of his life; of how an abandoned orphan of the French Revolution rose to become the chef of kings and king of chefs.

Lady Morgan herself was no stranger to being pointed out in the street. She was easy enough to recognise with her Celtic jewellery and scarlet cape – by those who could see her: she was barely four feet tall. She was in Paris researching the sequel to her 'bestseller', *France in 1818*, which would be titled, prosaically enough, *France in 1829*, and her subject that hot July evening was Carême, and a novel French cult: gastronomy. Potage à la Régence, Perche à la Hollandaise, Vol-au-vents à la Nesle, Salmon à la Rothschild: Carême's recipes were on

Marie Antonin Carême, 1784–1833, engraving
© Getty Images

everybody's lips because food was the thing to talk about in France in 1829. This was the first age of gastronomy – the first 'Age of Surfaces', as Lady Morgan's playwright friend Sheridan would have it – and the age when for the first time a chef became a celebrity.

-◀◀◆▶▶-

6 July 1829. Twelve hours earlier. A slight, ashen-faced man, looking older than his 45 years, breathed with difficulty in the early-morning Paris fug. His doctors, Broussais and Roque, were in disagreement about his ailment. But Antonin Carême knew. He had seen the same in older colleagues and friends; he was slowly dying from the poisonous fumes of a lifetime of cooking over charcoal.

With his weakening left arm, Antonin pulled himself into his carriage, which then followed the same route that Lady Morgan's would take later that day: by Napoleon's half-finished Arc de Triomphe, which Antonin had watched being built, and out on the new road to Boulogne-sur-Seine. Perhaps the air cleared a little as he left Paris behind, and his mind turned to the day's business: a formal dinner party for the Rothschilds in the orangery of their country château.

For a man who had once fed 10,000 people on the Champs-Elysées, this was small potatoes. Even so, work had begun the day before at the rue Saint Roch. Crayfish and brill, eel, cod and sea bass, quails, chickens, rabbits, pigeons, beef and lamb had been ordered from the Paris markets around

Les Halles – where Carême was a celebrated regular – along with specified offals: calves' udders, cocks'-combs and testicles, and the best Mocha coffee and truffles. Isinglass (fish gelatine) and veal stocks had been prepared, cream supplied locally, and the château's ice house restocked in expectation of Carême's arrival. The vegetables and fruit for the menu would be supplied from the Rothschild gardens. Antonin had also already begun work, with his young assistant Monsieur Jay, on the sugar-paste foundations of a table-length confection in the form of a Grecian temple, the Sultane à la Colonne.

At 7am a hush descended on the château kitchens as Carême arrived. The scullery maids and female staff curtsied and departed. Antonin took off the diamond ring from the index finger of his right hand, a gift from a grateful Tsar, and rolled up his sleeves. He put on a white toque, a fashion he had created himself, and smiled at Jay. Despite the heat, a dinner at the Rothschilds was always a cause for celebration.

The evening menu consisted of seven services, rather than courses as we know them now, offering 18 choices of dish to the dozen guests. Carême still catered to the tastes of his French employers for *service à la française*, where nearly all the food was presented on the table at the start of the meal, with only the soups and entrées literally 'making an entrance' hot. *Service à la russe* (the style Carême helped to import from Russia of serving plated courses in sequence as we might expect today) was a fashion too daring in 1829 for the socially ambitious Rothschilds.

Antonin explained the menu to the full-time staff – the pastry chefs, under-chefs, kitchen hands, table-deckers and footmen – and sent copies upstairs to the young Baronne de Rothschild and her husband, who were paying 8,000 francs per annum (around £150,000 in today's money) for Antonin's occasional services.

MENU

6th July 1829

Château Rothschild, Boulogne-sur-Seine

TWO POTAGES

Le potage à la Condé

Le potage Anglais de poisson à Lady Morgan

TWO RELEVÉS DE POISSONS

Grilled sea bass à l'Italienne

Cod à la Hollandaise

TWO GROSSES PIÈCES

Le quartier d'agneau à l'anglaise

La chartreuse, garnished with quails

FOUR ENTRÉES

Les petits vol-au-vent à la Nesle

L'émincé de filets de bœuf à la Clermont

Chicken à la maquignon

Glazed rabbit à la chicorée

TWO ROASTS

Chicken à la reine

Bacon-larded pigeon

TWO RELEVÉS DE PLATS DE ROT

Plombière nectarine

Oranges stuffed with marbled orange jellies

FOUR ENTREMETS

Les haricots blancs à la maître d'hôtel

Braised lettuce in consommé

Café Mocha fanchonettes

La Sultane à la Colonne

Coffee

The roasts and highly dressed *'grosses pièces'* would adorn the table as the guests arrived, along with the side dishes (*entremets*) including the centrepiece dessert, the Sultane à la Colonne. *Service à la française* dictated that everything be arranged in perfect symmetry. There were therefore two or four of each dish. Twice, the table would be completely reset with plates and cutlery. After the soup there would be a re-lay or relevés of hot fish, and after the roasts and entrées a new re-lay of cold desserts. The Sultane à la Colonne, a spectacular centrepiece of spun sugar in the form of a classical Greek temple, would remain on the table throughout the evening.

The kitchen day began in reverse order to the menu. With dessert. Antonin selected fruits for the puddings – a nectarine plombière (ice cream) and oranges stuffed with layered jellies. This necessitated a trip to the hothouses and walled gardens and a preliminary visit to the Orangery dining-room. It was a hot, close day, and Antonin sought local advice from the gardeners on the likelihood of rain. It would affect the jellies as well as the spun-sugar dessert. He instructed the windows of the dining-room to be shut, but for the internal fountains to play all day; the best that could be done in terms of air-conditioning. Work on the spun sugar would have to be delayed, and the isinglass ratio increased in all the jellies.

8am. Back in the kitchens the stoves were already stoked, and the blackened expanse of hob was filling with pans: yesterday's prepared veal stock, fish stock, partridge stock, and a velouté sauce to be thickened into sauce Allemande. Reductions of isinglass, of calves' udders, of clarifying sugar and nectarines, cochineal shells and melting Isigny butter were waiting for Antonin's arrival. He added more isinglass to the reduction, checked the aromatic herbs – marjoram, bay and thyme – in the wicker sieves at the side of the stock-pots, and passed on to the cooler confectionery room.

He shut the door behind him. The lubricious sweetness of almond milk, fresh-pressed through silk, cut through the citrus-oil smell of orange pith, exactly the contrast he had intended for the dessert. In one corner, a kitchen hand bent over the almonds and the straining silk; in another, Jay bored holes into oranges with a root cutter. Antonin took the tool from the strong hand of his intended son-in-law and demon-strated the deft incision; the fruit must not break. He left his assistant excavating orange flesh and briefly checked on work in his favoured domain: the pastry room.

Here, on marble slabs, two pastry cooks were crushing butter between layers of puff pastry to form '*fanchonette*' cases for the Mocha-cream desserts and the fly-away savoury cases that he had himself named 'vol-au-vents'. A double fold, a single fold. Six times. Twenty-four layers of butter and pastry. The ritual and the smell of Antonin's youth. He ordered more broken ice from the ice house and returned to the colder confectionery room.

There Antonin arranged the two dozen hollowed oranges, two inches apart, in a yard-diameter fruit colander filled with crushed ice. The cooling isinglass was brought from the kitchen along with blood-red cochineal, clarified syrup and the nectarine marmalade. Antonin poured the thickening isinglass alternately into the fruit juice and the almond milk. He added strained cochineal, drop by drop, and lemon juice from a coffee spoon, to the orange jelly, and poured the creamy blancmange or viscous amber juice into alternate orange shells. Throughout the day he would return, as if observing the offices of the monastic day, to the ice-cool of the confectionery room, testing each layer, one orange, one almond, adding more, building up the marble veins, as the ice dripped through the colander. In contrast, the plombière recipe proceeded simply. The strained nectarine marmalade, beaten with egg yolks and syrup, was set on ice, and left till later.

11am – and the kitchen resembled a field of battle. The acrid smell of burnt feathers and the co-mingling of blood and bile overpowered even the Mocha roasting on the stove top. Quails, the tiny infantry of the chartreuse mould, lay in ordered ranks, headless and tied. Flayed baby rabbits sat in lines on the central wooden table, surrounded by regiments of pigeons, cross-hatched with bacon-lard. Partridges and chickens were being chopped, washed, disembowelled and stuffed. The raw flesh of two boned chickens was being pressed through mesh, no easy task, by the brawniest of the kitchen hands, bloodied and sweating. Only the gullets and livid biles were discarded. The cocks'-combs and their testicles

– the size and shape of fish roe or overripe catkins – were set aside for the Nesle vol-au-vents. Bones and feet were placed in pans, to be reduced to thick glazing-stocks. The lamb, to be boiled in the English manner later in the day, had donated its brain and sweetbreads for the vol-au-vents, and the tenderest calves' udders, too, simmered to a pulp in cream, were being pummelled through a sieve. Antonin prodded, tasted, admonished, praised and glanced up at the large clock above the heat of the kitchen: seven hours until dinner. He called for more charcoal, and champagne.

Antonin drank very little, and then only the best. Three champagne bottles were opened. Two would be required for the fish soup, and nearly half a bottle for the sauce à l'Italienne. The rest would do for lunch. If some colour was returning to the face of the man once known as 'beau Carême', it was only the gathering heat of the day. He still looked older than his years, and ill. 'I sense that I've grown old very quickly,' he had remarked, but his close, dark eyes still sparkled with excitement in the reflected fire of a battery of copper casseroles.

Midday. Time for work to start on the 'extraordinaire' dessert: a columned sugar temple or Sultane. 'Spinning sugar,' Antonin explained to Jay, 'needs perfect preparation.' He selected two copper pans from the Rothschilds' batterie de cuisine, each four and a half inches wide by two and a half inches high, spouted and with a round handle of copper four inches long into which a wooden handle could be inserted for ease of spinning. The copper pans, freshly re-tinned inside and newly scoured with sand, vinegar and Breton salt, would be used in rotation for the sugar-spinning. Jay cleared the other pans from the stove for fear of anything touching the master's sugar and discolouring the contents with their heat. Two copper moulds, one domed, one flat, were prepared with almond oil.

Antonin took eight lumps of loaf sugar for each pan and four tablespoons of Seine water, filtered three times. He set them at the hottest part of the stove and watched them carefully. Jay stood behind him holding a cup of cold water and a small tin box, in which were two tightly sealed compartments. As the sugar began to boil, forming diamond-paste bubbles, Antonin reached behind him and Jay opened the box. Inside, Antonin's thin fingers felt for calcinated alum and then cream of tartar to fling, a pinch at a time, into the sugar-lava. The bubbles, the '*ebullitions*', became as large and bright as the eyeballs of a fresh cod.

Freezing his hand first in iced water, Antonin then plunged it straight into the boiling sugar, and back into the cold. A kitchen boy gasped – Carême's *pâtissier* trick never failed to impress. The sugar moved like soft wax between his fingers – it was not yet ready and would have to stay on the heat. To be soft like this it had been boiling at 121 degrees but needed to be hotter still in order to 'crack' and spin.

A few minutes passed and Antonin again plunged his hand first into freezing water and then molten sugar, and smiled. Next he took the sharpest knife that hung from his belt, dipped it into the top of the sugar-lava and then into the cup of water. He brought it straight out, cracking the crystalline sugar clean from the knife. He turned round to Jay and the others who had stopped work to watch. The master chef, knowing his audience was in the palm of his sugared hand, allowed himself his quizzical half-smile and announced to the kitchen in his thick Parisian accent, '*Cassé.*' The sugar was cracked and ready to spin.

Antonin now stood back from the stove with the first of the spouted pans. The other was pushed to the back of the range. He held the flat base mould at his waist and raised the pan to the height of his head and started to pour. The thread of sugar fell towards the mould, like a perfect skein of hot wax, and in one continuous movement Antonin laced it round. Up and down with the pan, gently round with the mould, until the inside was all alabaster sugar; as crisp as Limoges linen, as white as fleurs-de-lys. This would form the base of the temple cupola. The dome mould was next.

Jay set it spinning on a smooth wooden board at his master's feet. Antonin lowered and raised the pan to keep the thread of cooling sugar thin and constant. A little like the dome of Pavlovsk Palace, a touch of Carlton House, in spun sugar Carême could realise the palaces of his dreams and memories… But something startled him from his reverie; he had felt a draught, which could ruin the threading sugar. He ordered one of the kitchen hands to ensure that all the upper windows were firmly shut.

The heat rose gently. The coals sucked the air. Nine boilings of the sugar pans, attended by Jay, fed layer upon layer of sugar thread into the dome until it was ready to be gently detached from its oiled mould, glistening strong and imperious; a temple awaiting columns. Next, Antonin half-filled a large pan with red burning embers from the spit-roast hearth. The sugar pans were placed in this, inclined to one side. He wrapped a sheet of paper around the handles of two silver forks and dipped the double-trident into the cracked sugar and pulled it up to his eye-line. He dipped down again, and started to spin the sugar between the long fingers and thumb of his right hand. In the left, he held the sharp knife. Jay watched his master in awed silence, as he dipped and span, dipped and span, over and over. 'Spin,' he always said, 'so that it would be difficult to see the movement of the fingers.'

Eventually he was satisfied with the plaited rope of sugar – *cheveux d'anges*: angel hair. He laid the skein on baking paper and immediately cut it into seven-inch segments, repeating this dozens of times, until line after line of straight, clear sugar plaits dressed the table like the stems of Venetian wine glasses. Then he rolled bundles of them together, still warm, to form columns seven inches high and one inch in diameter.

From the scrapings in the bottom of the sugar pan, Antonin harvested warm, malleable sugar and fashioned it, like almond paste, into plinths and swags, column tops and pedestals. Next he took tongs to the burning coals and, seating himself at the main table, started to assemble his Grecian temple, his Sultane à la Colonne, by burning the sugar ends, till they blistered against the coals in pin-sized bubbles, pressing each part to the blistered side of another, and holding for the two seconds of adhesion. Voilà! Plinth to column. Column to architrave. Architrave to dome. Dessert.

In the confectionery room, Jay, along with the table-decker and an assistant chef, had assembled the silver salver and the first layer of the dessert: a rockery of hand-painted almond paste. The message came for them to join Antonin in the kitchen. They all plunged their hands in crushed ice, and dried them on napkins as they walked the few yards to the kitchen. Aware of the quick, dark eyes of their master, they lifted the delicate temple by the arches of the cupola, the columns in turn lifting the translucent base, and then moving as one, breath held, walked carefully back towards the confectionery room. Once placed on the marzipan, there would only be one more precarious move for the dessert: to the table.

Later, Antonin would garnish the temple with meringues filled with vanilla cream, choux glazed with caramel and dipped in sugar grains, chopped pistachios and small white pastries. He would add some fallen columns in the Romantic style, a little 'moss', made from almond paste dyed green with spinach and pressed through a sieve, and, on the column which would be nearest the most honoured guest, write in royal icing her name: 'Lady Morgan'. He knew when to flatter.

By mid-afternoon, the soups were almost complete. To further honour the influential writer Antonin had created a new champagne fish soup in her name. It was an elaborate English-style fish consommé, with floating escalopes of eel, brill and sole, perhaps to remind her of Ireland, and tiny egg-like quenelles of whiting that were pressed, Antonin insisted, between the finest silver coffee spoons. Extravagant garnishes were being prepared for the plate rim: crayfish tails, oysters and truffles cut into petals. The second soup was simpler and more classically French – potage à la Condé – from the recipe book of Carême's hero, the Prince de Condé's chef, Vatel.

Nearby on the stove in a low bain-marie was the sauce à l'Italienne for the sea bass; a reduction of champagne and velouté with herbs. The fish were already prepared and on ice, the cod was stuffed with rock salt, its flesh scored three times with deep incisions towards the head.

4pm. The heat was intensifying in the kitchen. Antonin prepared the roasts on spits and the cauldrons for boiling meat and fish. He called for more ice to keep the desserts cold in the confectionery room and the pastry room cool enough for the unbaked pastries. The floors were wet with melted ice, thickened with sawdust from the Rothschild timber mill, running with flour and seasonings, feathers and fat – till the kitchen boy came back on his rounds, brushing it all into a sluice drain.

Carême's attention went next to the assembly of the quail chartreuse and vol-au-vents à la Nesle, and to the delicate sauces to accompany the fish relevés and entrées. Carême's chartreuse, flaunting the Lenten origins of the dish, would contrast layers of cabbage, lettuce and spinach pressed in deep moulds with an unholy army of little quails. The vol-au-vents would be roofed with tiny morsels of forcemeat, small enough to flick off with the tongue and melt with the lightest of pressure to the mouth's roof. Ten parts panada (French bread sauce) to eight parts puréed calves' udder, to six parts pressed chicken flesh: more pounding and straining, more yolks and cream, a hint of nutmeg, a paring of truffle, rolled in coffee spoons, poached in consommé, glazed in velouté. The cocks'-combs, the sweetbreads, the truffles and lobster tails that hid below in the vol-au-vent shells served only to prove that nothing could surpass the delicacy of perfectly judged Carême forcemeat.

6pm. The table-deckers in the dining-room had been at work for over an hour. A white damask cloth covered the oval table, falling beyond the floor as was the fashion. In his youth Antonin recalled men of taste using the tablecloth itself as a napkin. No longer. The neoclassical simplicity of the Orangery dining-room, an oblong pavilion of Grecian marble, was mirrored in the fashionable white porcelain place settings. A large, flat tablespoon only was laid at each place, on the right, for the soup; the Rothschild crest facing up, the spoon's head facing down. On the left, starched napkins were folded into the shape of water-lilies. Jay and two table-deckers, piloted by Antonin, manoeuvred the Sultane à la Colonne from the confectionery room through the Orangery to the dining pavilion. A footman, his feet bound in protective padding, stood on the table to help guide it into its central position, the column dedicated to Lady

Morgan facing the place to the baron's right. Antonin decorated the Sultane further with laurel and orange leaves and left.

6.15pm. In the cool of the confectionery and pastry rooms, Antonin tested mayonnaise in iced sauce boats, sliced half of the oranges into quarters, revealing the marbled layers of jelly and blancmange, and arranged the rest with laurel leaves in two pyramids. To complete the plombière, he folded whipped cream into the half-set nectarine syrup and piled it like an alp above an ice-chilled silver pedestal. For now, the iced desserts remained in the cool of the confectionery room.

6.30pm. The scene on his return to the kitchens was very familiar to Carême:

Imagine yourself in a large kitchen before a great dinner. There one sees twenty chefs at their urgent occupations, coming and going, moving with speed in the cauldron of heat. Look at the great mass of burning charcoal, a whole cubic metre for the cooking of entrées and another mass on the ovens for the cooking of the soups, the sauces, the ragouts, the frying and the bains-maries. Add to that a heap of burning wood in front of which four spits are turning, one of which bears a sirloin weighing forty-five to sixty pounds, another a piece of veal weighing thirty-five to forty-five pounds, the other two for fowl and game. In this furnace everyone moved with tremendous speed, not a sound was heard; only I had the right to be heard and at the sound of my soft voice, everyone obeys. Finally, to put the lid on our sufferings, for about an hour the doors and windows are closed so that the air does not cool the food as it is being dished up. And in this way, I passed the best days of my life.

6.45pm. Antonin added lemon juice and butter to the sauce à l'Italienne, noted the milk-steamed cod-flesh sloughing away from the cuts, fried bread for the potage à la Condé, arranged braised lettuce in consommé, opened oysters for the soup, garnished the chickens with pastries, the fanchonettes with miniature meringues, the lamb with glazed onions and the chartreuse with quails' eggs. The guests were entering the dining-room.

It was seven o'clock as Lady Morgan took her place next to James de Rothschild. Amid the hubbub of German, Italian, English and French, the footmen entered with the two silver tureens. They took the soup plates from the guests, replacing them with warmed plates and their choice of garnished potage. As the soups were served, Lady Morgan later wrote, silence fell.

In the kitchens, there was no such calm. The hollandaise was decanted into two identical sauce boats, and the mayonnaise nested in ice. Although the roasts and the *grosses pièces* were already on the table, the meal proper was now about to begin. The fish were sent out with heated plates and the first new set of cutlery: a knife and three-pronged fork to replace the large, flat soupspoons.

As the guests in the Orangery were admiring the cod and sea bass, in the kitchens work began on finishing the entrées.

The vol-au-vents were assembled; sweetbreads, cocks'-combs, testes, lobster and truffles surmounted with forcemeat balls, all glazed with the sauce Allemande. The rabbits were removed from skewers and dressed with glazed chicory, the thin beef fillets were alternated on silver salvers with tenderest rabbit, and onions were stuffed with chestnuts à la Clermont.

Meanwhile, at table, Rothschild himself carved the roasts. On to the same plates on which they had had the fish, the guests helped themselves to the elaborate *grosses pièces* and side dishes – the monumental displays of pressed quail and cabbage which subsided to the left and right; the sauces, the delicate seasonings, mixed on the painted plates.

Word was sent to Carême that the entrées should be delayed. In the Orangery, even Lady Morgan was at a loss for words. The colours, the freshness astonished her: 'To do justice to the science and research of a dinner so served would require a knowledge,' she wrote, 'of chemical precision.'

The next wave of food, the entrées, arrived with the footmen: the vol-au-vents, the beef, the chickens and rabbits dressed with chicory. In the kitchen, for the first time in many hours, Antonin sat down. Presently he would garnish the chilled plombière for the final reset of the table. The Sultane was already wilting in the heat of the freshly lit candles as night fell round the Orangery, and the footman began warming coffee cups and scurrying from the wine cellars. The glory of Antonin's art, so long in the preparation, was brief.

In the dining-room, Lady Morgan blushed. Only she,

she realised – among a gathering that included Rothschild's political cronies and even the composer Rossini – only she had had her name etched out in dedication on Carême's sugar temple. She asked to meet the chef.

Antonin was already getting into his carriage when word arrived. He would have to attend 'milady' in the hallway of the château. An hour passed. By the time they met, Antonin had been at work for 18 hours. His head span and his arms ached. He was courteous but brief.

'He was a well-bred gentleman,' observed Lady Morgan later, quite wrongly as it happened. 'And when we had mutually congratulated each other on our respective works, he bowed himself out, got into his carriage, and returned to Paris.' The dinner was one of the last formal meals he ever cooked. 'Our work destroys us,' Carême once said of the life of a great chef. 'Our only duty, after cooking, is to record and publish, or if not we will suffer such regrets.' Three years later, he was dead.

NECTARINE PLOMBIÈRE

as served to Lady Morgan at Château Rothschild

Reserve some 'perfect' nectarines for garnish. Boil fifteen peeled, stoned nectarines with six ounces of sugar into a 'marmalade'. Press through a sieve. Leave to cool. Put the yolks of four eggs, a spoonful of rice flour and three glasses of full cream milk (nearly boiling) in a pan. Stir over a low heat with a wooden spoon. When it starts to thicken, remove from heat, stir till smooth, and then let simmer, very gently, stirring, till it has the consistency of custard, after which add two ounces of pounded sugar and a grain of salt. Place in a large cold pan, with the cooled marmalade, and set on ice. Just before serving, stir in a 'plateful' of thickly whipped cream. Serve on a silver pedestal as a 'rock' or in sugar-glazed vol-au-vent cases, or in cups made from marzipan.

Antonin Carême

CHAPTER 2

Pastry Boy

*You are more the son of our times than you are the
son of your own father.*

Prince Charles Maurice Talleyrand to his chef, Antonin Carême

aris, Left Bank slums, 1783. Sometime between the
Paris première of *The Marriage of Figaro* and the
first flight of the Montgolfiers' balloon – an age of
revolution and of ascent – a boy was born to Marie Jeanne
Pascal and Jean Gilbert Carême. Just when is less clear. The
records of Carême's birth, and that of any siblings, were
destroyed in 1871 – coincidentally along with the last of his
preserved desserts – during the bombardment of Paris in the
Franco-Prussian war. Carême, precise to the point of pedantry
with his recipes, probably didn't know his exact age himself.
He seems to have been the 16th child of the prodigiously
fecund Marie Jeanne and Jean Gilbert. He may have had as
many as 24 siblings.

He was born, he said, in a timber-yard shack off the rue du Bac near where his father laboured – an area now occupied by the Bon Marché department store, but which in 1783 was the Left Bank's dankest slum. His parents seem to have been poor, too, in political judgment and christened their 16th child in honour of Queen Marie Antoinette at a time when royalist sentiment in Paris was as scarce as cheap bread. So Marie Antoine Carême was known to everyone else, and ever afterwards, as Antonin.

For little Antonin, Paris during the Revolution was not a fine dawn in which to be alive. Neither consistency nor bitterness characterised his later thoughts on a childhood which undoubtedly scarred him, but about one fact he was always clear: in the autumn of 1792 he was taken from his Left Bank home and was abandoned.

In all the history of Paris, a city plagued by street violence, the last months of 1792 stand out for their horrors and turmoil. There were massacres – even of children – at the Paris prisons and the Tuilieries palace, and heads and body parts were paraded on spikes through the streets. There are accounts of traumatised foreigners and vagrants – like Antonin – pleading for mercy before being beaten to death. 'Terror' was to be the 'order of the day', Robespierre had announced, purging the old regime through violence and changing every standard, from the length of weeks to the times of meals. Crowds gathered daily for the new spectacle of La Guillotine; thousands were arrested or displaced.

And in this throng was one small – and doubtless terrified – ten-year-old boy.

Antonin's father, possibly with consideration for his other children, and seemingly with the prescience and sang-froid of another contemporary father of foundlings, Jean-Jacques Rousseau, took young Carême to the busy Maine gate of Paris and left him with these words: 'Nowadays you need only the spirit to make your fortune to make one, and you have that spirit. *Va petit!* – With what God has given you.'

Antonin did not wander for long the streets which Madame Tussaud later described as bloodstained and littered with 'appalling objects'. The crowds around the Guillotine were famously hungry, and Antonin was taken in by a busy cook who offered him bed and board in exchange for skivvying.

The best recipes, like genesis myths, feel familiar even when they are truly unique: Moses was found by a princess; Carême was rescued from the Terror by a cook. Carême certainly enjoyed telling this story. It became part of his mystique. And it was repeated and embellished by his employers, and given suitable literary spin by no less than Alexander Dumas in his exhaustive *Grand Dictionnaire de la cuisine*. Carême's was, it seems, the perfect Revolutionary and Romantic background: the child who would create order and triumphant classicism in the kitchens of France emerged from the gutter and the turmoil of the Paris Terror. Naturally, Napoleon would approve.

Indeed Carême's very name, with its Lent and Carnival associations in French and its caramel confusions in English (he did *not* invent caramel, or crème caramel, no matter what they used to say at the Brighton Pavilion), has led some to suggest that certain details of his provenance were more fiction than fact. For along with the perfect Romantic and Revolutionary background, Carême seems to have had the ideal name for his chosen profession. His future employer, Talleyrand, spoke with typically arch diplomacy when he said Carême was 'more the child of his time than the child of his own father' – just possibly he was a foundling. Just possibly Talleyrand was hinting that, like the painter Delacroix, he believed Carême was maybe one of his natural children. Or just possibly Carême's own story was true.

What we do know is that, sometime between Louis XVI and Marie Antoinette's arrest at a Sainte Ménèhould pig-foot restaurant (as *their* story goes) and the queen's last meal (bouillon and vermicelli) en route to the Guillotine in October 1793, young Antonin began his kitchen apprenticeship. He was employed as a lowly kitchen boy in a *gargotier*, or chophouse, with the cook who had found him.

The world of Paris cooking into which Antonin had stumbled was in as much turmoil as its politics. On the streets and in cookbook prefaces, in medical texts and in fashionable conversations, even in a hit play, de Beaunoir's *Blanquette et Restaurant*, a debate raged over 'ancient' and 'modern' cookery. Was fine food a pernicious luxury of the royalist past or France's greatest democratic art? Was the heavy spicing of the previous century to be replaced with a purer, codified style?

Should food be served almost as a buffet – *à la française* – or in the modern democratic style of plated courses – *service à la russe*? At the centre of the debate was a novelty of Paris life – the restaurant – and Antonin's first obsession: soup.

The French Revolution is often credited with having given birth to the restaurant. Although there had long been taverns or chophouses in France, Parisian 'restaurants' before the Revolution did not serve food. They served only soups – bouillon and potage – to lift the spirits and relieve the pervasive respiratory ailments of the fashionably 'sensible', as coffee had done for an earlier generation. Going to a restaurant was considered, literally, a restorative (*restauratif*) act.

Prior to 1789, only certain privileged caterers (*traiteurs*), besides the taverners, had the right to cook and serve food for the many Parisian households that did not have kitchens, and these caterers were protected by restrictive guild practices. But all of this changed with the Revolution. The guild restrictions were overturned, freeing up the catering economy in Paris, while a market emerged, as new regional deputies flooded into the capital to take up their posts. At the same time, on the domestic front, the former aristocracy's chefs – the original *cordons bleus* – found themselves unemployed. And many of these now opened establishments that served food, and called them 'restaurants'. Soup, nevertheless, remained key to every menu.

Carême grew up at a time when soup was a fashionable health-food, and later in life he was categorical that every meal should start with one. For him this was philosophy and medicine as much as it was cookery. Soups were democratic; they allowed each meal to start with a communal act. They were almost a philosophical statement; part of the return to simplicity that was the style of the age. He called his soup-based menus '*nouvelle cuisine*' – in what was probably the first instance of the phrase being used to describe a revolution in food.

The several hundred soup recipes attributed to Carême range from the purest consommés to floating armadas of seafood 'quenelles' with garnishes which took days to prepare. Some of them were cited for their specific medicinal qualities: one recipe involving a purée of snails and four dozen frogs' thighs was said by him to relieve coughs. Every soup, however, was meant to rejuvenate the palate, and enliven the spirits of those at the table in readiness for the rest of the meal. They were, in almost every sense, aperitifs.

And yet, fashionable though they were in the 1790s, soups would never have made Carême's name – any more than working as a restaurateur would have done. The *gargotiers* (chophouse owners), like the one with whom Antonin first trained, were pretty near the bottom of the Paris food chain. Further up there were *traiteurs*. But the real stars of post-Revolutionary French cooking were not the restaurateurs, they were the confectioners and *pâtissiers*. And it was as a confectioner that Carême would first come to the notice of the gourmets of Paris.

In 1798 he left the unnamed *gargotier* who had found him near the Maine gate and began an apprenticeship with Sylvain Bailly, a *pâtissier* on the rue Vivienne. It was a fortuitous move. Some art forms survive revolution better than others and the evanescent luxury of confectionery never fell victim to political attack. In fact, quite the opposite. Young Antonin's Paris, according to contemporary diarists, was awhirl with ridiculous fads, with fashion victims like the *Incroyables* and *Merveilleuses* (the male and female dandies), and with pineapple ices and pastries. Since the collective loosening of stays that had greeted the fall of Robespierre in 1794, Paris had been reinvented as the 'City of Light' – and capital of food.

Bailly's, on the rue Vivienne, just behind the bustling Palais Royal, was well placed to take advantage of the fashion for indulgence, and the years from 1798 to 1802 – during which Bonaparte rose to power within the Directory and then effected a coup to create himself First Consul – saw also the rise of Monsieur Bailly and his ambitious apprentice.

While many of his contemporaries were fighting for young General Bonaparte in Italy, the teenage Antonin was sifting flour and growing yeast blooms from potato peels. He lived on the premises, never far from the heat of the kitchens or the sudden demands for iced *génoise* cakes or *gâteaux pithiviers*. And, though his master released him briefly to study with the affectedly named Monsieur Rose at the *pâtissier-restaurant* on the rue Grange-Batelière, his world was centred on Bailly's and the Palais Royal.

He thus found himself cooking in the most vibrant neighbourhood of post-Revolutionary Paris. The colourful local crowd who breakfasted on Antonin's pastries ranged from ambitious revolutionary politicians like Simon Bolívar, who drafted South American constitutions in lodgings just by Bailly's, to the stars of the nearby Comédie-Française, and even the prostitutes who now plied their trade in the gardens of the Palais Royal where the Sun King had once played as a child. For in the 1790s the former royal residence became a hotbed of political and sexual intrigue, and a seedbed of culinary invention, and saw the birth as a result of a new concept in city living. Under the Orléans Duke Philippe 'Egalité' (the only Bourbon prince to support the Revolution), the sprawling Palais Royal had been opened up to businesses of every sort: clothes shops, cafés and bookstalls. Many of the most successful new-styled 'restaurants' also opened in the palace arcades and spilled out into the gardens. Antonin delivered pastries to these restaurants and saw at first hand the birth not only of the 'shopping arcade' but also a vital part of the food myth of Paris: café society. All around the Palais the talk was of philosophy, fashion, food and sex: what the world has come to expect of Paris. The virginity of a Parisian adolescent was most often lost in the late 18th century in this heady atmosphere – above a Palais restaurant if he had the money; in the gardens if he had less. Such was the tale of a young soldier called Napoleon; very likely it was Antonin's too.

From these adolescent years in the pastry kitchens, however, came the beginnings of Antonin's ill health. An apprentice was not free for long from the demands of pâtisserie: the four-hourly checks on the warming croissant dough, the knocking back, the folding in of butter and flour through arm-numbing stone mangles; and all in the most uncomfortable of surroundings. Andrea Palladio's neoclassical architecture had not been good to 18th-century city cooks like Carême. Palladio had advocated building kitchens *under* the house and even below street level. Bailly's shop may have had tall, airy windows, but the confined subterranean space that was Carême's world was dark and damp and filled with dangerous carbon-monoxide fumes from the charcoal. Antonin once wrote:

The cook too often spends his working life underground, where the false day of artificial light enfeebles his eyesight, where condensation and drafts accelerate rheumatism and where his life is miserable. If kitchens are on the ground floor, the chef is healthier, but even so he often only sees the four walls and his own reflection in polished copper and all he breathes is charcoal fumes and steam. There you have it – my life as a chef!

If most of his working days were nasty, brutish and long, he did occasionally find that his afternoons were free. And he would spend them at the library. On the opposite side of the rue Vivienne from Bailly's was the Bibliothèque Nationale and its print room. The adolescent Carême – a self-taught reader – became bookish and serious. In summer, the natural light in the high-windowed Cabinet des Gravures allowed reading into the early evening. And here, usually on Tuesdays and Fridays, Antonin would research ancient and foreign food. His first passion, though, and doubtless his respite from cooking, was classical architecture. He studied Palladio, Tertio, Vignole and the architecture of India, China and Egypt as it was then understood in the *Voyages Historiques et Pittoresques* and *Maisons de Campagne*. He later wrote of this as an intensely studious and inspiring period of his life, his small frame huddled at 'the table of learned men, admiring monuments and the detail of architecture'.

Antonin always argued that food was very like architecture, the final construction in both cases relying upon a balance of well-organised elements. He developed a painter's – even a scenic-artist's – eye for visual impact and extravagant dramatic decoration. 'I believe architecture to be the first amongst the arts,' he proclaimed, 'and the principal branch of architecture is confectionery.'

He copied in ink – and then created in pastry and marzipan, in sugar-paste and spun sugar – the ruined castles and hermitages, temples, pyramids and fountains he had seen in the Bibliothèque. He visited the Déssert de Retz, the park of classical follies outside Paris, and read in translation the first 'Gothic' novels then fashionable in Paris – Horace Walpole's *Le Château d'Otrante*, and the works of the French imitators of

Ann Radcliffe like François Guillaume Ducray-Duminil. His mind's eye was filling with the frivolities – and portentousness – of the Romantic landscape.

Monsieur Bailly, unsurprisingly, was less interested in Antonin's artistic education than in his growing reputation as a confectioner. Nevertheless, he made a play of encouraging him in his studies at the library, for which Antonin was always grateful. 'It gave me the confidence,' he said, 'to attempt the centrepieces being asked of me; what use my drawings if I could not reproduce them in pâtisserie?'

These centrepieces or *extraordinaires* – which Antonin nicknamed 'extras' – have not survived into the modern cook's repertoire. The most closely related descendant would be the tiered and iced centrepiece of a traditional Western wedding; a creation which is more about display and occasion than about taste, and made to look anything but what it is: a cake.

The centrepiece had an impressive pedigree in France, though. The most famous *extraordinaire* was the christening cake for the grandson of Louis XIV in 1682. Given by the governor of Guyenne, it was fashioned out of almond paste, pastry and clockwork, and both depicted and animated the labour pains of La Dauphine and the baby Duke of Angoulême's entry into the world via a marzipan vagina.

Fortunately for Carême, with his passion for architectural extravagance, the '*pièce montée*' continued to dominate post-Revolutionary table-settings. And these would soon become his speciality. Some of his designs – the Parnassus Fountain for example – took several days to assemble. Often built on rocky outcrops made from meringues or *croque-en-bouche*, his folly-desserts were usually created with confectioners' pastry or durable and heavily salted *pâte morte* and *pâte d'office*. The segments were glued together with mastic and gum arabic (acacia tree resin) before being elaborately decorated with spun sugar and icing. Most were several feet high. One rotunda with palm trees had 'six columns, the top of which were decorated with white flowers made from *pâte d'office* or marzipan or light pink icing. The palm leaves were pale green icing, and the roof of the rotunda masked with spun sugar… the floor of the rotunda was made with nougat and the base garnished with petits madeleines and lemons.' On other occasions, using salt-pastry, nougat, spun sugar and marzipan, he created Athenian ruins with fallen columns, Russian hermitages, ships in sail, turning globes, harps, lyres, Roman temples and Chinese pagodas.

These luxuriantly decorated *extraordinaires* were not meant to be consumed, though they could be. More often, only a few elements of the design could be eaten – the fruits on the trees, for instance – while the main elements were kept and recycled for another occasion. Many of Carême's *pièces montées* – or at least the inedible portions of them – survived the chef by a generation.

Pastry work and confectionery is detailed and ordered, at odds with the flair and disregard for precision more often associated with a great and innovative chef. But Carême managed to reconcile the two worlds. The regularity of the classical architecture that he studied at the Bibliothèque Nationale and the chemical precision of the yeast recipes he learned with Sylvain Bailly never left him. The man who would later be grandly titled the 'Palladio of Pâtisserie' was always, at heart, a pastry boy.

Carême's time at Bailly's gave him the first three ingredients in the recipe of his subsequent success. It was there that he learned his craft as a *pâtissier* – he was *'premier tourrier'* by his 17th birthday – and there that he created the earliest of the *extraordinaires* based on the drawings he had made in the Bibliothèque Nationale, for which he first became known in Paris. But it was there, too, that he came to the notice of another gourmet resident of the rue Vivienne: Charles Maurice Talleyrand.

VERMICELLI SOUP

**The last meal of Queen Marie Antoinette
before her execution.**

Prepare consommé using one whole fowl but no beef bones. Add 12 ounces of Italian vermicelli. Leave to simmer for 25 minutes and serve in a tureen filled with a pint of blanched peas or the tips of half a bunch of asparagus, blanched to a fine green, with a little sugar and blanched chervil.

BOUILLON D'ESCARGOTS ET DE GRENOUILLES POUR LES TOUX SECHES

Broth of snails and frogs, for Coughs

Take 12 snails and four dozen frogs' thighs and sweat them over a low fire. Pound them, and re-boil them with two pints of water, adding the whites of four leeks, six small turnips cut into pieces and two spoonfuls of pearl barley. Skim the broth, reduce it by one third and pass it though a sieve. Use one half in the morning, coloured with saffron, and the remainder in the evening.

Antonin Carême

CHAPTER 3

Breakfast at Talleyrand's

The discovery of a new dish does as much for the
happiness of mankind as the discovery of a new star ...
Tell me what you eat and I will tell you what you are.

Jean Anthelme Brillat-Savarin (1755–1826)

C harles Maurice de Talleyrand-Périgord (1754–
1838) had four great passions in life: conversation,
politics, women and food. Before and after the
Revolution when he lived on the rue Vivienne, three minutes
by sedan to breakfast at the Palais Royal, he was an inner
member of the Duc d'Orléans's circle. So, too, was the
writer Choderlos de Laclos, who has left us, in *Les Liaisons
dangereuses*, such a vivid portrait of their time. When the
prim Misses Fanny and Susanna Burney were introduced
to Talleyrand, one writer later remarked, it was as if the
sisters of *Sense and Sensibility* had walked straight into *Les*

Liaisons dangereuses. It was this world that Carême – till then a bookish innocent himself – came to know through the wily politician who befriended him.

Talleyrand, uniquely, held high office in every administration from the Court of Louis XVI, through the Directoire, the Consulate and Napoleon's Empire to the restored Bourbon monarchy and the constitutional monarchy of Louis-Philippe. Along the way he measured his political life in meals. Rejected, like Antonin, by his parents, he was forced to enter the church before turning to politics, rising to become Bishop of Autun, where he became notorious for organising elaborate banquets to curry favour with his clergy. Later renouncing the priesthood in favour of secular politics, and facing excommunication for swearing allegiance to the anti-clerical French constitution of 1791, Talleyrand gamely wrote to the Duc de Biron, 'Come and console me, I am forbidden fire and water so we shall eat only glacé foods and chilled wine.' After the Revolution he was to be found, briefly, in Philadelphia, cooking mutton with Madame de la Tour du Pin in impecunious exile. But by 1797, on the night before he finally returned to office as foreign minister under the Directoire, he was muttering, '*Une fortune immense, une fortune immense*' about his new prospects as he ate with Madame de Staël and Joséphine Bonaparte's former lover Paul Barras. By contrast, he affected impartial guilelessness at a simple meal at Meudon on the eve of the momentous coup d'état that would bring Napoleon to power in 1799, but when asked what he needed to secure French rights at the 1814 Congress of Vienna, he replied, quite simply: 'More casseroles.'

Seemingly totally unencumbered by scruples, the Abbé Talleyrand 'would sell his soul for money and he would be right to, for he would be exchanging dung for gold,' spat the politician Mirabeau. (It should be pointed out that Mirabeau's mistress was at that very moment being seduced over dinner by the famous gourmet. Yet Talleyrand and Mirabeau subsequently became firm friends. Even those predisposed to dislike him rarely could in person, especially after enjoying his – and Carême's – hospitality.)

'Attempts to arm oneself against his faults were in vain. His charm always penetrated the armour and left one like a fascinated bird in the gaze of a serpent,' said Madame de la Tour du Pin. The Countess Kielmannsegge agreed: 'God gave you [Talleyrand] the choice between snake and tiger and you chose to be an anaconda.' Antonin adored him.

Talleyrand, of course, did not actually come in person to the pâtisserie on the rue Vivienne. He might well have noted Carême's window displays from his sedan-chair window – the mountains of nougat, meringues, *beignets* and *flanets*. But it was Boucher, Talleyrand's maitre d', who alerted his sweet-toothed master to the young *pâtissier*.

The career of Boucher tells us a good deal about the changing world order. Before the Revolution Boucher had been chef to another aristocrat-gourmet, the Prince de Condé. He was thus proudly able to boast that he was a direct successor of the famous Vatel, a previous chef in the Condé household, known for his vanilla-laced Chantilly cream and for committing suicide in the hot panic of an ill-planned banquet for Louis XIV. When it appeared that there would be insufficient seafood supplies for the royal table, Vatel had thrown himself upon his sword, shouting: 'I have lost my honour – this is a blow which I cannot bear – my mind is spinning – I haven't slept for a dozen nights!' The fish arrived as Vatel died, but the myth of the tempestuous genius-chef was born. As Antonin, made of more pragmatic stuff, remarked: 'Poor Vatel did lose his head somewhat.'

After the Revolution, Citizen Boucher had found a route back to the centre of Parisian gourmet life by accepting terms of employment – after both their returns from exile – with Talleyrand. And, by the mid-1790s, as Talleyrand's political career required more and more entertaining, Boucher found himself on the look-out for useful freelancers. He had noticed the work of the talented young pâtissier further up the rue Vivienne and, in order to be able to call on his exclusive services when required, he now encouraged Antonin to leave his post at Bailly's and move to Gendron's where he would be in a better position to undertake freelance commissions. This Antonin did. Though still not legally of age, he was canny enough to strike a deal with Gendron whereby he could easily be released from the quotidian duties of pastry-making for special commissions for his *pièces montées*. And these special commissions came mainly from one household: Talleyrand's.

An unlikely association – of acolyte and mentor – developed between young Antonin Carême and the snake-eyed politician to whom Boucher introduced him. Talleyrand and Carême shared much common ground. Both bore the psychological scars of being abandoned by their parents. Talleyrand's had disinherited him as a result of his lameness, forcing him against his will into the Church. Both would forge careers in fast-changing 'media' – diplomacy and gastronomy – and through diligent application and selectively deployed charm, would make as many enemies as friends en route. And both, while paying lip-service to the ideal of a legitimate monarchy and the glory of France, would in time be happy to take posts under the Napoleonic empire and the Russian army of occupation. Over 30 years of acquaintance, each would heap praise on the other.

By 1798 Talleyrand's household was divided between the rue Vivienne and the new ministry of foreign affairs at the Hôtel Galliffet in the now fashionable Faubourg Saint Germain on Paris's Left Bank. Only a year before, the French government – which had requisitioned the palace during the Revolution – had given it to the ministry of foreign affairs, in effect to Talleyrand. It was squeezed uncomfortably between the tiny rues Varenne and de Grenelle but its Palladian grandeur would have sat easily on the banks of the Tiber – indeed it now houses the Italian Cultural Institute of Paris. It was a palace Talleyrand could be proud of. When Antonin first saw it, the dining-room had just been re-gilded by the former royal architect Bellanger and new windows fitted throughout to replace those broken in the Revolution.

When he started working for Talleyrand in the newly termed '7th arrondissement', Carême was returning to within yards of his birthplace. The area had changed a good deal since then. There had been a building frenzy on the Left Bank in the years leading up to 1789 – the unfortunate Galliffet himself had only just completed his Hôtel when the Revolution led to his demise. It is even possible that Jean Gilbert Carême had worked on the construction of the palace where his son would one day work. Yet even though he was now so close to where his family had once lived, there is no record that Antonin made any contact with them. He was moving in more exalted circles – or rather underneath them.

In the arched basement of the Hôtel Galliffet – now the Italian embassy's library but then the kitchens – Antonin became part of a culinary team which cooked for some of the most glittering events of the Directoire, Consulate and First Empire.

To begin with, he had responsibility mainly for the *extraordinaires*. On the floor above the kitchens, in the neoclassical dining-room designed by LeGrand, with its *trompe l'œil* skies and priceless floor-to-ceiling mirrors, his 'extras' vied with Talleyrand's famous collection of Baccarat crystal for the attention of Napoleonic high society. The novelist Madame de Staël was a frequent guest. So, too, were the political writer Châteaubriand, the poet Arnault, and Napoleon and Joséphine themselves.

Food was always central to Talleyrand's entertaining. In honour of Joséphine's birthday, before she was Empress, he threw a dinner where only the ladies were seated. Their consorts, including the diminutive First Consul, stood behind the ladies and served. Years later, from his exile on Saint Helena, Napoleon would remember that night as one that had marked the 'high-water mark' of Directoire refinement. In fact, Napoleon himself was bored by food. If a meal lasted for more than 20 minutes he was heard to remark: 'Ah, power is beginning to corrupt.' Talleyrand, by contrast, was utterly in thrall to good eating – corrupting or otherwise.

The household were given less than a week to arrange the birthday dinner; the list of workers hired in reads more like a stage crew than a kitchen. Painters, artificial flower arrangers, sculptors and printers were all engaged, and dozens of extra kitchen staff. All the rooms were perfumed with amber, and the ladies were requested to dress in classical style. The celebrated couturier Madame Guermon created dresses in the fashion now associated with Joséphine and the Directoire – 'nudités gazées' in crêpe and gauze and linen. And for the first time in Paris, that night, on the floors above Antonin's kitchen, a new sound was heard: the waltz.

'Throughout dinner,' wrote Lady Frances Shelley of another occasion at the Hôtel Galliffet, 'the conversation was about food. Each plate gave rise to a commentary and the antiquity of each bottle of wine furnished the opportunity for an eloquent dissertation. Talleyrand analysed the dinner with the interest and seriousness accorded to a political problem.'

The earnest young scholar in his kitchens had much to learn from such an erudite connoisseur as Talleyrand. 'The most noble title you can give a rich man,' said Antonin, 'is that he has merited the title of a gourmet, and one who shares fine wine and good food with his friends is the most noble of all.'

But, for all his famous munificence, Talleyrand's parties were not always unalloyed successes. Of another dinner at the ministry of foreign affairs, the Countess of Bessborough wrote to her daughter, Caroline Lamb, 'I never saw anything so magnificent – the apartments beautiful, all perfumed with incense. As soon as the seventy-eight people – of which the company consisted – sat down, an immense glass [mirror] at the end of the room slid away by degrees and soft and beautiful music began to play in the midst of the tingle of glasses and *vaiselles*.' This mirror revealed the Carême buffet – the *grosses pièces* and *extraordinaires* – while the entrées and relevés were self-served from the table. 'The dinner was, I believe, excellent,' Lady Bessborough concluded, 'but from some awkwardness in the arrangement it was very difficult to get anything to eat.' So much for *service à la française*!

At the Hôtel Galliffet Antonin began to learn the evolving rules of banquet cooking. Where at Bailly's, in the stone-cellar calm of the pastry room he and his colleagues had only had to focus on one thing – the production of perfect pâtisserie – at the Hôtel Galliffet they had to create an entire banquet involving hundreds of dishes, many of them hot. A window display is one thing, but traditional *service à la française* is another. Increasingly, Carême came to believe that the most dramatic effects of traditionally arranged and displayed meals, where almost everything was displayed at once, did not necessarily serve the interests of the food itself; while engaging the eye they often left the tongue and stomach disappointed. Dishes ended up cold, ruined in the move from display to plate or simply inadequately shared around – as Lady Bessborough commented. It was a problem that he would return to later in detail.

As Carême grew in experience, Talleyrand began to recommend him to his influential friends, some of them, it might be said, in need of advice on how to spend elegantly their newly acquired wealth. Among those for whom the term *nouveau riche* was invented was Pauline Borghèse, the sister of Napoleon and new owner of the neglected château of Neuilly. The first time Carême visited the château he found the pastry oven had not been lit in two years. He gives a gruelling impression of what followed to create a series of 'extras' for the First Consul's sister.

It took from ten in the morning on the day of arrival until midnight to heat up the oven. Carême, who had three assistants for such work, spent the time in-between readying the pastry and the complicated dyes required to colour an *extraordinaire*. Large amounts of spinach were needed to stain the pastry and the icing just the right hue of delicate 'empire' green.

The work of the next day began at 4am. *Crème pâtissière* was made on this second day, and pistachios trimmed and chopped. Choux pastry was in the oven by nine, along with brioches that together would form the grottoes and rockeries around the pastry buildings, and presumably be more obviously edible. By midday Carême's famous *babas* – made with rye flour and soaked in Hungarian wine – were also baking.

All day cakes and pastries came in and out of the oven, and it was only by three in the morning in the middle of the second night that the pieces were ready to be glued together. The cooks then took a break, had some soup, a glass of wine, and went to bed. Antonin woke everybody two hours later so that the elaborate construction could be dressed and iced and the foliage created on the plants and vines. All the pâtisserie was ready by one o'clock.

At four o'clock Carême started decorating the minor desserts and ice creams. In the years following the Revolution, dinner had gradually moved from being served mid-afternoon

These pièces montées, *or* extraordinaires *(simple by Carême's standards), feature fruit made of marzipan on pedestals created out of sculpted pastry*

to mid-evening; for most cooks the extra time this afforded was an advantage, though for Carême it meant finishing the confectionary in the full heat of the day. By seven o'clock everything he had been working on – 16 *pièces montées* in the case of Pauline Borghèse's soirée – was finally placed in line for dinner, some 57 hours after his arrival at the château.

At this time, Antonin's working life was split between Monsieur Gendron's pâtisserie, the kitchens of the Hôtel Galliffet and one-off freelance jobs for wealthy Talleyrand contacts like Napoleon's sister. Though he frequently passed near the slum where he was born, he was now as far removed from the world he had come from as were the Réunion vanilla ships on the Paris quaysides. Back and forth across the stinking Seine, we might imagine him, a young man in the first flush of success, in the traditional unbleached white of the *cordons bleus*, or perhaps the old-style 'aristocratic' livery that was reappearing in fashionable post-Revolutionary households and restaurants. Having grabbed cooked oysters from the *traiteurs* who, now that dinner was served so late, were providing a new meal, 'lunch' (*déjeuner à la fourchette*), Antonin would have been stopped on the barred Seine bridges for the checking of papers – a last vestige of the Terror. He would have been let through without question, however: he was carrying the crest of the notorious foreign minister – together with his precious cargo of sugar-craft.

PETITS GATEAUX ROYAUX

Roll two thin sheets of puff paste. Spread a pot of pineapple jam on one (peach, plum or apricot may be used), and cover with the other sheet. Cut into ovals with a two and half inch oval cutter, and turn upside down. Take six ounces of pounded vanilla sugar and mix with some egg white, work it with a silver spoon into an icing rather thin. Spread over. Leave the cakes to dry for half and hour before putting into slow oven to brown to a reddish tint. Or ice with 6 ounces of scraped chocolate, mixed with 4 ounces of sugar and the white of an egg. Bake in a gentler oven. If they are attended to, although they may be of a brown colour, they will not be unhandsome.

Antonin Carême

CHAPTER 4

Gastronomy:
A Cult in Want of a Priest

*The upheaval that has taken place in the redistribution
of wealth as a natural result of the Revolution has
transferred old riches into new hands. As the mentality of
these overnight millionaires revolves around purely animal
pleasures, it is believed that a service might be rendered
them by offering a reliable guide to that most solid part of
their affections. The hearts of the greatest number of rich
Parisians have suddenly been transformed into gullets.*

Grimod de la Reynière, *Almanach des Gourmands* (1803)

astronomy – the 'art of good eating' as termed
by the Académie Française – emerged in the first
decade of the nineteenth century. Just as the
English novel set the tone for manners and mores for the
emerging British middle classes, the post-Revolutionary

French looked for guidance not so much on how they should behave but on what and how to eat. From 1803, Grimod de la Reynière's *Almanach des Gourmands* – and later the *Manuel des Amphitryons* (from 'Amphitryon', the eponymous gourmet in Molière's comedy) – set the standard on Paris food and French cuisine. As a tourist map to the new restaurants and also a paean to the craft of men like Carême, the *Almanach* was widely read in London, and helped to foment the myth of gourmet Paris. Without it, Carême could never have become such a star.

Grimod de la Reynière, eccentric host and lawyer, deformed since childhood by the attack of a ferocious pig, lavished love in an unloving world on food. He has reason to be considered the first restaurant critic, and in the *Almanach* he both celebrated and codified the new ideas about food ('If stews are too spicy and over-seasoned, it is time to call an apothecary for the cook') and with his readers began the search for the individual artist-cooks who might justify their adoration. He wrote: 'The most consummate cook is alas seldom noticed by the master, or heard of by the guests who, while they are devouring his Turtle and drinking his wine, care very little who dressed the one or sent the other.' We ignore great cooks at our peril, de la Reynière warned; they make or break an occasion no matter whether the host is 'as witty as Voltaire or as warm-hearted as Beaumarchais'.

The influence of de la Reynière and the gastronomes on the career of a chef like Carême was intensified in 1802 by the Peace of Amiens, which brokered peace with Britain and for the first time in years allowed an excited new influx of travellers to Paris. Cosmopolitan travellers, such as the artists Turner, Farington and the Cosways, were among the first to arrive, and all were struck by the number of restaurants, the quality of the food and the 'great number of crowded tables, no cloth as such, an oiled canvas, and under each plate, a napkin to tuck in to a collar'. Before the Revolution, there were less than 50 restaurants in Paris. By 1814 the *Almanach* was listing more than 3,000. Even Marie Antoinette's thatched hermitage at Le Petit Trianon had been turned into a restaurant, with a dinner menu boasting hothouse peaches and costing six livres (or five shillings) a head.

Why, then, did Antonin not become a restaurant chef? He certainly knew the restaurateur Beauvilliers, whose establishment, La Grande Taverne de Londres, was a first stop for visitors who had read the *Almanach des Gourmands*. (Beauvilliers's choice of name for his restaurant reveals, ironically, how Parisians at first considered restaurant-dining to be quaintly and attractively in the *style-anglais*, just like novels, neckties and constitutional monarchy.) But Carême never seriously considered running a restaurant himself.

Though ambitious, he was a pragmatist. Despite the fact that he had already been working for a decade, he was still not even legally of age. He was guided, too, by the example of that most fickle of French '*girouettes*', or political pinwheels, Talleyrand. Antonin knew that to nail his colours to a restaurant, favoured by one political faction or another, was more risky in troubled times than cooking privately for whichever elite was in power.

Extraordinaires, his speciality, were by their very nature evanescent, peripatetic – and profitable. They were the swash and buckle of catering – a young blade's dandy-craft – the sort of thing that caught the eye of the new gastronomes. Unconstrained by the daily responsibility of running a restaurant, Antonin could be more creatively extravagant, could have more autonomy, and be more resilient to the changeable political winds. He also looked set to make more money.

In the winter of 1803 to 1804, using the capital he had made from his brisk trade in *extraordinaires*, Carême opened his own pâtisserie on the newly redeveloped rue de la Paix, just along from the Place Vendôme. Talleyrand may have helped with the money and the lease; he and Napoleon were keen to revivify the area after the ravages of the Revolution and the disturbance of building the nearby rue de Rivoli. If so, Talleyrand's investment seems quickly to have paid off. The business did well, with Carême's crisp almond *'croquants'* the big sellers, as well as his already sought-after puff pastry.

Carême's invention of the vol-au-vent – so light it literally 'flew-on-the-wind' out of the oven – is traditionally ascribed to this time and place. He was also responsible at this stage for the fashion of the 'gros meringues' that are still today a pâtisserie and dessert staple, usually in the form of a later adaptation, the Pavlova. It was Carême, at the rue de la Paix, who was the first to pipe meringue through an icing bag, where previously, even at Le Petit Trianon in the hands of no less a cook than Marie Antoinette, meringues had been formed between two spoons.

Carême ran the business on the rue de la Paix until 1815 or 1816, though it is unclear how much day-to-day involvement he had as his importance rose to the dizzy heights of cooking for Napoleon's family and at Talleyrand's Paris and country residences. But during that time the pâtisserie was invaluable for two reasons. Firstly as a base, a kitchen that was his to command, where he could create the *extraordinaires* that graced the tables of the rich. And also as publicity. The window of Carême's on the rue de la Paix became a celebrated Parisian landmark, illustrated in gastronomic guides like de la Reynière's *Manuel des Amphitryons*. It was still trading under the name of Carême as late as 1863.

Had Antonin not been as restive as he was creative, he might perhaps have settled into life balancing the books on the rue de la Paix; a businessman, confectioner and *traiteur,* part of the scene described by de la Reynière. Instead, he travelled a different route, and one not so far from the career open to modern chefs. He wanted to learn more, and to learn by example. Under the tutelage of the greatest chefs of the day, whose kitchens he shared as a freelance confectioner, he concentrated on further expanding his repertoire and his reputation. Although the Talleyrand household had first call on his services, he also cooked for Napoleon's sister Caroline and her husband Joachim Murat before they quitted Paris for the throne of Naples, and frequently for a noted Paris gourmet, Monsieur Lavalette at the Saxon Embassy.

Carême chased these commissions – to create 'extras' – on the basis of the chefs' reputations rather than their employers'. 'It was under Monsieur Richaut, the famous sauce cook of the house of Condé,' he later wrote, 'that I learned the preparation of sauces, during splendid festivities held at the Hôtel de Ville [for Napoleon's wedding], and under the orders of Monsieur Lasne that I learned the best part of cold buffet preparation... I saw a great deal, I made valuable observations and I have profited by them.'

Just as the new Napoleonic elite was relearning the old manners of the court from those like Talleyrand who had known Versailles, Carême, too, was learning from the former *cordons bleus*, who found themselves once again in demand. 'I worked with Avice and Tiroloy [formerly chefs for the Duke d'Orléans], Feuillet and Lecoq [who had worked for the late king], Robert, Richard, Bardet, Savart, from whom I learned more about soups, and Riquette [famous for his roasts].' Carême also worked with the most renowned of the old guard, the chef Laguipierre, who later froze to death on Napoleon's disastrous retreat from Moscow.

After volunteering his time in the kitchens of these older chefs, Antonin was able to use what he learned, and gradually transform himself from being solely a pastry chef into a general freelance dinner chef. His credo was simple, even if the occasions were not: 'The best way for a gourmet to appreciate his dinner,' he said, 'is for him to have it served to him by his cook.'

He began by cooking small, intimate dinners for paying patrons, doubtless featuring one of his famous desserts, but 'simple and exquisite', composed of 'only four entrées'. Monsieur Lavalette began to employ Carême to create whole meals on his own, and at the Barbe-Marbois household also, presided over by the American gourmet Madame Barbe-Marbois, Antonin was given complete freedom to experiment as a chef, rather than just a pastry cook.

'I was utterly free to compose menus. It was then [at Madame Barbe-Marbois's] that I could do most to address the issue as I saw it; the union of delicacy and order and economy. The guests were very assiduous at these dinners, usually members of the Senate, academics, famous officers; all connoisseurs.' The Marquis de Cussy later noted the perfect scale for these experimental Carême dinners: 'More than the Graces but less than Muses' – in other words, a dinner party for four to nine gourmets.

Antonin worked all over Paris at this period, and he later cited both happy and unhappy experiences of clients of varying taste and breeding. He was passionate about food and feasting and his disdain for those who did not share his passion – in the kitchen or dining-room – was withering: 'The rich man who is miserly only eats to live, lives his life in mediocrity, and dies in it too.' / 'A rich man who does not appreciate a good cook will never know ineffable joy.'

The young chef's worst censure, though, was reserved for ignorant guests who failed to realise that, with cooking, timing is everything: 'The guest whose tardiness delays the meal,' he said, 'should have the dining-room door slammed in his face.'

VOL-AU-VENTS PUITS D'AMOUR

Fountain of Love Vol-au-vents

I give great preference to these, being crisp and having the advantage of being light and of easy digestion with an interior containing a greater portion of garniture than any other cake that I am acquainted with. Dip the vol-au-vent cases, in the shape of diamonds, boxes or rounds, in caramel and then in chopped pistachios, fill with cream, flavoured with violets, or vanilla crême Chantilly (in the style created by Vatel) with a fine strawberry or preserved maraschino cherry on top.

Antonin Carême

CHAPTER 5

Château Valençay:
A Year in the Loire

Advice to young chefs: young people who love your art;
have courage, perseverance ... always hope ... don't
count on anyone, be sure of yourself, of your talent and
your probity and all will be well.

Antonin Carême

By 1803 Napoleon, the First Consul, had ambitions for himself and for France that were clearly imperial. In 1804 he colluded in the assassination of the Duc d'Enghien, son of the Prince de Condé and a contender for the French throne, and this was swiftly followed by his and Joséphine's coronation as Emperor and Empress. While shivering crowds warmed themselves on free hot food from the Tuileries palace kitchens, the exhausted imperial couple dined alone in their new crowns. Talleyrand remained circumspect about the future: 'If he lasts a year, he will go far.' Carême, however, was to benefit greatly from Talleyrand's ability to ingratiate himself with the new 'Imperial' court.

Talleyrand had been at dinner with the Duchesse de Luynes on the night of the murder of the young duke. In the early hours of the morning he had looked up coldly from the hazard gaming table to the clock and informed the guests that 'The house of Condé is no more!' The next day he ordered Carême and his staff to organise a celebratory banquet at the ministry of foreign affairs.

All Paris wanted to fête their new emperor. And before Napoleon left Paris to campaign in Germany, the newly appointed 'Imperial' generals threw a ball for him at the Salle de l'Opéra. Talleyrand recommended Carême, who created over 30 towering '*suédois*' – eye-catching layers of fruit in syrup presented in moulds with aspic and jelly. The Opéra *suédois* were the talk of Paris for days after the departure of the new Emperor's army – according to Carême at least.

That the Emperor was as impressed as everyone else by the *suédois* seems unlikely, however, given his famous disinterest in food – 'Only if you want to eat quickly,' he once said, 'eat *chez moi*.' His unwillingness to eat in public was supported by his glamorous consort. The Empress Joséphine detested formal, public dining for reasons of intimate vanity: the 'Decaying Creole' was anxious to conceal her appallingly bad teeth.

'You must receive, instead of me,' Napoleon said to Talleyrand before leaving Paris, acknowledging the growing importance of diplomatic banqueting. The Emperor insisted that Talleyrand entertain at least four times a week in his place, with no less than 36 guests at each dinner. He went further. 'I want you to buy an estate where you can receive the diplomatic corps *brilliantly* so that foreigners will want to visit you. I want an invitation [to Talleyrand's] to be a recompense for ambassadors of sovereigns with whom I am happy.' Talleyrand did not need to be asked twice. He bought Château Valençay with 1,600,000 francs of government money.

-≪◆≫-

TRIPS TO TALLEYRAND'S château probably took Antonin, just turned 21, out of Paris for the first time in his life. Valençay, between Berry and Châteauroux in the southern Loire, was several days by road from the capital. But certainly his first arrival there – with Talleyrand – would have been worth the difficult journey. The windows and the plane-tree-lined approach of the medieval château, white and steeply tiled, were lit up with candles and torches. In the semi-enclosed courtyard beyond the towering white gatehouse, the country servants arrayed themselves with the Limousin countryside as a backdrop. 'It made a very pretty tableau,' wrote the Duchesse de Dino, a frequent visitor. Carême would later say that he had never been happy outside France, but by this he meant Paris – and Valençay – for they were all the France he ever knew. Under Talleyrand, and with Carême in its kitchens, the renovated and redecorated fairytale château became the French nation's projection of its ideal. Nowhere could provide the chauvinistic Frenchman with better proof that France is made in the image of Heaven.

In the afternoon the Valençay guests would walk in the Gâtines forest or to the ruined château at Veuil, where Talleyrand would arrange for Carême to provide *déjeuner sur l'herbe*, and for musicians to hide in the turrets and play. In the evening, guests gathered in the Grand Salon among the spoils of Napoleon's generosity – Canova's *Paris*, alabaster vases and paintings by the Italian masters. The strategy worked a treat. The Diplomatic Corps would later report back on Talleyrand's courtly art of conversation, his elaborate and old-fashioned dress and etiquette – and his young chef's exquisite cooking.

Antonin would spend most of the day with the evening meal in mind. Long before the guests had departed for morning Mass in the, apparently, malodorous local church, Carême would be at work in the large, high-ceilinged kitchens. Valençay is built on a hillside, allowing access to the kitchens at ground level, even though they were below and to the side of the dining-room. There is still a dumb-waiter connecting the kitchens and dining-room which Carême is said to have

Empress Joséphine (1763–1814), was born in Martinique. The 'Decaying Creole' was older than Napoleon and embarrassed by her rotten teeth. For this reason, she never smiled with her mouth open, and abhorred formal, public dining

introduced – but this, like so much that links Carême to Valençay, may be more legend than fact.

For several years while Napoleon fought for control of Spain, Valençay served as a gilded cage for the deposed Spanish royal family, who were forced to term themselves 'guests' at Talleyrand's dinner table while Bonaparte's brother ate Valenciana paellas in their Madrid palace and termed himself Spain's 'king'. The sojourn of the Spanish princes led to further improvement of the château: the royal prisoners were made to pay 200,000 francs for works including a hydraulic pump to send water gushing to the kitchens, and to Carême's vegetable garden.

In many ways, Valençay was the ideal backdrop for Antonin – with marvellous kitchens, able to take full advantage of France's best country produce, within minutes of well-watered herb gardens and positioned beneath an airy dining-room, the whole presided over by a wealthy gourmet.

Early each day at the château, if we are to follow the legend, Antonin was summoned to talk to Talleyrand on the subject of dinner. They met in the small room on the first floor reserved for Talleyrand's ablutions and his most honoured guests. Here they would talk for up to an hour. 'Never was talent so happy or highly placed,' said Antonin of this impressive scene: the chef and the powdered, braided gourmet-politician in a boudoir which still contains several hundred volumes, and was decorated then with works by Titian, Holbein and Rembrandt. 'Talleyrand and his table were furnished with grandeur and with wisdom,' Carême recalled, omitting to mention that this favoured morning conference – at Valençay as at Gallifet – was also in the company of Monsignor's barber.

These breakfast meetings yielded an important new concept, for Carême and for the cookbook genre. As an amusement and challenge for them both, and in the spirit of a Napoleonic code for the kitchen, Talleyrand now set his chef a Herculean task. He was to create a different menu for every day of the year. It was to cater to Lenten observance and make use, where appropriate, of the great variance of French seasonal produce: 'The man who does not love September,' said Carême after this forced reliance on nature's immediate bounty, 'does not deserve to eat well.' The spectacular seasonal menus Carême created are preserved in his *Maître d'hôtel* published in 1822. Many of the meals seem designed for Valençay, where Antonin would have been more in touch with the seasons than when the markets of Paris were at his disposal, though in truth he was clearly never at the château for an entire year.

Let us take as an example from the 365 possibilities: a summer evening at Valençay, Antonin's birthday – which is to say the birthday his family celebrated – 8 June. He gives a suggested menu for ten to 12 people.

Next page: Château Valençay, which Talleyrand bought with 1,600,000 francs of government money, to be able to 'receive the diplomatic corps brilliantly' on Napoleon's behalf

MENU

8th June 1806 Château Valençay

TWO SOUPS

Potage of puréed peas with small croûtons

Game consommé

TWO FISH RELEVÉS

Little trouts au bleu

Eel in Bordeaux wine

TWO GROSSES PIÈCES

Noix de veau with glazed onions

Chicken à l'ivoire in aspic

FOUR ENTRÈES

Thinly sliced beef filets à la Clermont

Chicken supreme quenelles

Filets of young rabbit à l'Allemande

Fried chicken à la Saint-Florentin

TWO ROASTS

Roast lapwings

Young turkey in watercress

TWO RELEVÉS

Milan flan

Cherry gâteau

FOUR ENTREMETS

Steamed lettuce

Artichokes fried à la Provençale

Raspberry jellied moulds

Baked lemon soufflés

IT WOULD HAVE been a complicated meal to prepare, but would have been neither heavily creamy nor overburdened with strong flavours. Clearly served *à la française*, almost everything would have been available after the soup 'course', with the relevés and the entrées served hot from the oven. As always in *service à la française*, the dishes would have been divisible by two, and arranged around the table symmetrically for the convenience of the guests. Yet the predominance of entrées, with only two prepared '*grosses pièces*' (savoury centrepieces), hints at the slowly changing fashion of the times. It is not a long journey from this menu to *service à la russe* as practised in France and elsewhere today.

Dinner was served even later at Valençay than in Paris, where one English traveller had complained of the 'abominable habit of dining as late as seven in the evening'. It was considered a particular joy of the château to ride in the gardens at twilight, and Talleyrand invariably had government business to complete before the last mail left for Paris.

Talleyrand was a stickler for old-fashioned manners at table. He served Carême's meats, the *grosses pièces* – once they had been removed for carving – strictly according to rank: 'Your Highness would you do me the honour of trying some beef? Your Grace, would it please you to have some beef? My Lord, may I serve you the beef? Monsieur: beef.'

The menu for 8 June was relatively carnivorous, with eight choices of meat, as well as the two fish and assorted sweet and savoury side dishes, but only two vegetable dishes. And it would have been a long meal. As the Marquis de Cussy later wrote, Talleyrand, who was so sharp in Napoleon's cabinet, was less brilliant by the end of dinner – which at Valençay could last late into the night.

In the servants' garret in the great round tower of Valençay, Antonin was unlikely to be slumbering as his master finally limped to bed. The strange hours of the chef can lead to unusual sleep patterns and fractured lives. It was not unusual for him to work over 50 days at a stretch without a single day off. The Sabbath, like Christmas, is no day of rest in professional kitchens. And besides being under constant physical strain, he showed signs of an increasingly compulsive personality: he worked at feverish pitch on his *extraordinaires*, and he was plagued by insomnia and increasingly troubled relationships. It might be that his genius was allied, as so often, to a mildly manic-depressive nature, and he complained bitterly of jealousy and pettiness in the kitchen. He would burn out, according to one later writer, 'from the fire of his genius and the flames of the *rôtisserie*'. There was at least some truth in this: it was the charcoal that got him in the end, as it did so many chefs.

The move from the cool of the pastry room to the cauldron of the kitchens, be they at Valençay or Paris, was a necessary one as Carême's career broadened. But, like any cook of the time, he suffered for his art. 'We must obey,' said Antonin, 'honour commands – even though physical strength fails. But it is the burning coals that kill us!'

Ambitious, solipsistic, even narcissistic, Carême was not an easy man to get along with. Equanimity was in short supply among chefs, what with the fumes, long hours – and the flies. The summers at Valençay were hot and still, while the Seine in Paris attracted a wealth of unwelcome insect life. In an attempt to keep the flies at bay, Antonin pioneered the use of sugar solutions in jam-jars as improvised traps, and used to tally the daily cull: 1,215 was his record. It is hard to believe that the busy young chef counted flies late into the night, and perhaps the details of his boast are to be taken with more than a pinch from the *salière*. But even if he gave this gruesome task to some unfortunate Valençay kitchen boy, it points equally to an increasingly obsessive character.

SOUFFLÉ AUX FRAISES

The classic soufflé was Carême's invention.

Hull a large basket of fresh strawberries, crush them and press them through a sieve. Mix a pound and half of powdered sugar with 18 stiffly beaten egg whites. Stir in the strawberry purée. Pour the mixture into a croustade of eleven inches diameter surrounded by buttered papers... put the soufflé in a moderate oven and give it a good hour's cooking. When it is ready to serve, put red-hot cinders on a large metal baking sheet. Take the soufflé from the oven and place it on the hot cinders so it stays puffed. Meanwhile cover it with powdered sugar and glaze it with a red-hot iron, then carry it very quickly to the dining-room. Set it on the platter, which should be covered with a fine damask napkin. Remove the paper holding up the soufflé and serve at once. Soufflés of raspberries, gooseberries, mirabelle and greengage plums the same.

Antonin Carême

CHAPTER 6

Napoleon's Wedding Cake

Et bon, bon, bon
C'est un garçon
Vive Napoleon!

Paris street chant, 1811

Betsy Patterson of Baltimore had hopes of ending 1807 as a princess of the French Empire. Having captured the heart of the underage Jerome Bonaparte and married him, she suffered from the delusion that she could win round his brother, the Emperor, by 'the enchantment of my beauty' alone. Napoleon had other plans. Betsy and Jerome were hastily divorced and Jerome was married off instead to Princess Catherine of Wurtemberg. Their wedding was intended by the fledgling regime as a testament to the status of the new imperial dynasty – though it would be quite outclassed a few years later by that of the Emperor himself.

Talleyrand suggested that his protégé, Carême, should participate in the preparations for the wedding banquet. In the meantime, the Elysée-Napoléon was transformed in the Romantic style, with bridges, thatched cottages, pavilions and grottoes, all illuminated by candle flame and fireworks. Antonin was tremendously impressed. Mainly he loved the ersatz architecture, but he revelled, too, in his first experience of state banqueting. It was, he said, the best catered affair he had ever witnessed.

The man in charge of operations was the imperial maître d'hôtel Monsieur Robert, but in the kitchens the chef Laguipierre was in control. Laguipierre had shared a kitchen before with Antonin and appreciated his particular culinary skills. He put him to work with another 'freelance' chef called Riquette on the cold service: the formal French table arrangements that would counterpoint Laguipierre's hot entrées and *assiettes volantes* (the innumerable side dishes that all but literally 'flew' by).

Antonin and Riquette created first 24 large joints to be served cold at the wedding breakfast, then 14 pedestals holding six hams each, six galantines, two stuffed boars' heads and six veal loins in aspic. There was also beef in aspic, veal brains dressed with aspic borders, foïe gras, chicken galantines and a whole array of fish. The salmon was bordered with a pink butter sauce; the eels with a pale green shallot sauce. The chopped aspic jelly so favoured by Carême as a border was similarly delicately coloured in the neoclassical hues favoured by the Empress Joséphine.

A personal triumph, the occasion marked Antonin's first outing as a court cook. He always spoke of it as one of the 'happiest, best organised and most refined marriages' – meaning, of course, the marriage of food and setting, rather than that of Jerome and Catherine. It was also the beginning of one of his few friendships: he and the older Riquette would seek each other out in the years to come, in St Petersburg and London, and warn each other of the employers to avoid.

At 25, Antonin had become a well-known figure among the chefs and gourmets of Napoleonic Paris. He was handsome, his hair cut and tousled forward in the fashionably Byronic manner, which flattered, as intended, a hairline beginning to recede at the temples and a face which was open, clear-eyed and purposeful. He was described as slight, and a slight eater. Only in one drawing, a Cruikshank cartoon, does he look as if he ever partook of his sugary creations and this was probably drawn without reference to reality. He was febrile and gauche, sometimes a little pedantic, doubtless a little petulant, with a distinct tendency to be over-sensitive; common characteristics of a child with, in Antonin's case, good reason to feel abandoned. He never seemed confident of the love or even esteem of others. But he had looks, great prospects, charm when he chose, and wit, and in 1808 he met a captain's daughter a year younger than himself and asked her to marry him.

One of the few dates that can be attached to Carême without the aid of a menu card is 18 October 1808 – the date of his wedding. In the small Paris study of the Notary

Monsieur Hua, not far from the noisy building site that would be Napoleon's Arc de Triomphe, Antonin married Henriette Sophie Mahy de Chitenay.

'Marie Antoine Carême, citizen, do you consent to take as your lawful wife Mademoiselle Henriette Sophie Mahy de Chitenay, here present, to keep faith with her, and to observe conjugal fidelity?'

'Citizen,' said Antonin, 'I do.'

'Mademoiselle Henriette Sophie Mahy de Chitenay, citizen, do you consent to take as your lawful husband Marie Antoine Carême, here present, to keep faith with him, and to observe conjugal fidelity?'

'Citizen,' replied the captain's daughter, 'I do.'

With the simple words 'the law unites you' the boy from the gutter married his well-to-do fiancée. She was the daughter of Charles Mahy de Chitenay and his wife Henriette. Captain Mahy de Chitenay had more than an aristocratic name to join to Carême's. His daughter Henriette Sophie brought with her 14,000 francs in dowry. The groom, for his part, brought only 3,000 francs to the marriage. Although Antonin would soon be commanding significant sums of money, he was not yet a wealthy man. Still, he was able to set up home with Henriette Sophie in some style (3,000 francs was roughly equal to ten times the average annual wage of a Parisian labourer at the start of the 19th century).

An intriguing mystery smudges the margins of the certificate that the two parties then signed. When Henriette

Sophie died, 20 years after Antonin, her second husband is noted as one Antoine Michel Guyet. He also signed the register that autumn day in Monsieur Hua's study. He was Antonin's best man.

To add to the confusion, Antonin's only child, Marie, born some years later, was not Henriette Sophie's. Her mother was Agathe Guichardet. If Agathe was Antonin's second wife, he fails to mention either divorce or remarriage, and on his 1833 death certificate Henriette Sophie is listed as his widow. What, then, happened to the young lovers, Antonin and Henriette? Perhaps, like Napoleon, Antonin found his first marriage to be barren. Perhaps Agathe was his mistress and Marie was illegitimate. Perhaps Antonin fell foul of that familiar tale of marital breakdown for the overworked and frequently absent – a spouse's affair with a 'best friend'. He never wrote a word on the subject. Most likely he did divorce – for whatever reasons – and remarry.

Carême's idea of celebrity was a long way from ours: in his cookbooks, he would later disclose the minutiae of his professional life, intimate conversations with royalty if they polished his reputation, and the menus, guests and ingredients that made up his working days. But about his personal life he revealed nothing.

Meanwhile, his 'career' went into overdrive. Talleyrand had been advising Bonaparte for some while that the heir necessary to secure the Napoleonic regime would not be forthcoming from his marriage with Joséphine. And

Napoleon now reluctantly agreed to divorce his 'barren' empress in order to marry, at Talleyrand's suggestion, a teenage Austrian archduchess: Marie Louise Hapsburg. This wedding was to link Carême's name more closely than ever to that of Napoleon.

The painter Alexandre Dufay depicts the wedding scene on 2 April 1810 as a closely modelled replay, somewhat tastelessly, of the wedding of Marie Louise's ill-fated great-aunt, Marie Antoinette. Huge bowls of fruit adorned the tables, in the style of the previous century, and 3,000 sausages and free wine were distributed to the crowd. There was a series of balls and receptions which Antonin heavily criticised for their careless extravagance and vulgarity. 'I have never seen extras done worse,' said Antonin, 'or things worse organised than then... *Tout va clopin-clopant!*'

But his is a biased account. Antonin himself had been contracted to cook for the main civic reception at the Hôtel de Ville de Paris, and this event, he tells us, was by far the most stylish. What he does not relate is exactly what he cooked. Probably this is because it was an extravagant *extraordinaire* in the style that had made him famous, a style of which he was now tiring, and possibly also because when he came to write about it, Napoleon's was no longer a name to drop. Frustrating though it is for us now, Antonin had his eye on current fame rather than posterity so he must be forgiven for failing to give the recipe of what could have been his greatest claim to fame: Napoleon's wedding cake.

The union was blessed, almost immediately, by the conception of a child (Napoleon said of his wedding night that his bride 'liked it so much she wanted to do it again'). The baby would be named at his birth in March 1811 the 'King of Rome' (which was news to the Italians), but for Talleyrand, Carême and the Napoleonic establishment, this was an even greater cause for celebration: the imperial dynasty, and the alliance with Austria, looked a little more secure.

News of the birth was carried by the recently invented semaphore from Paris to Turin within five hours and to Venice within seven. Carême himself in Talleyrand's kitchens cheered with the rest the 22nd cannon fired from the nearby Tuileries gardens, signalling the arrival not of a girl (worthy of a 21-gun salute), but a boy (worthy of 100). The christening celebrations were as lavish as those conducted for his parents' wedding. Carême was contracted to create a confectionery suitable for the baptism of an Italian infant-king:

A VENETIAN GONDOLA

(an Italian-themed extraordinaire)

The Venetian Gondola is made of confectioner's paste masked with sky-blue sugar icing. It is placed on a convex pedestal, four inches high in the centre and two round the outside, covered with white spun sugar so as to imitate the waves of the sea. The pavilion is composed of eight columns masked with rose-coloured sugar icing, the draperies are of sky-blue confectioner's paste and yellow spun sugar. The cupola, the sail and the small pendant are of spun sugar; the mast is masked in the same way as the gondola, and the tackle is formed with white spun sugar. The whole is encircled with a border of middle-sized meringues with coarse sugar and filled with cream. The gondola, too, may be filled with meringues, large truffles boiled in champagne or with small casks of almond paste filled with preserves.

Antonin Carême, *Le Pâtissier royal parisien* (1815)

Carême was never 'Napoleon's chef' as would later be claimed. Nevertheless, his creation of *extraordinaires* for the imperial nuptials and baptism provided two vital credits for his curriculum vitae. They were the reason that the fanciful British Prince Regent later claimed that he had employed the vanquished Emperor's cook.

Over the years, the Talleyrand household, to which Carême was linked by bonds of loyalty and patronage rather than pay and contract, grew in keeping with the minister's wealth. The 20-strong kitchen staff at the Hôtel Galliffet in 1804 had doubled by 1808 when Talleyrand, newly ennobled by Napoleon as the Prince de Bénévent, briefly took up residence further along the rue Varenne at the Hôtel de Matignon. And in 1811 the household again moved, to the palace on the corner of the rue Saint Florentin and the Place de la Concorde that is now the American Consulate. By then there were upwards of 80 men and women working in the kitchens.

The staffing and the new location made life easier for Carême. Hôtel Talleyrand was only a few minutes from Carême's pâtisserie-home on the rue de la Paix – a walk which entailed passing the Place Vendôme and its towering new centrepiece, the Colonne de la Grande Armée, formed entirely from melted Austrian cannon. The building site that Napoleon had made of Paris in the 1810s had led to street congestion, and quite how Carême moved his *extraordinaires* around Paris is a matter of enjoyable conjecture – he mentions barges and tumbrels. One thing is certain, where once he had needed identity papers from the foreign ministry, now the name 'Carême' was sufficient to allow ease of passage everywhere. In some circles, Antonin's name was as renowned as his master's and he was becoming as useful to the old rogue of Parisian politics as Talleyrand had once been to him.

Antonin, 27 years old, married and in possession of some means and greater fame, lived already in a world as removed from the squalor of the rue du Bac as truffles from turnips. But he would have remained a far lesser name to history, except among chefs, had his various masters' careers progressed as smoothly as his. Napoleon was on the slide. And so, potentially, was Talleyrand.

SMALL CHESTNUT BISCUITS

Sold, when in season, from the
rue de la Paix pâtisserie

Roast 36 chestnuts in the cinders, clean and remove from them every particle coloured by the fire. Pound together six ounces of chestnuts with two ounces of butter and pass through a hair sieve. Mix together four ounces of flour and three ounces of pounded sugar and make a hollow in their middle, into which put two ounces of fresh butter, the chestnuts and an egg and grain of salt and form into a smooth paste. Form into the size of walnuts and lay on a slightly buttered baking tray. Glaze all with egg. Brown them in a medium oven, and then put in a slow oven for a short time to become crisp.

Antonin Carême

CHAPTER 7

The Russians in Paris

*'How can we fight the French, Prince?' said Count
Rostopchin. 'How can we fight against our teachers
and divinities? The French are our Gods; Paris is the
Kingdom of Heaven.'*

Leo Tolstoy, *War and Peace*

W hen news reached Paris of Napoleon's disastrous
retreat from Moscow in 1812, Antonin was
appalled: 'A hundred thousand men and *fifty*
chefs!' Of the 20-strong personal household of the Duc
de Narbonne, many of them known to Antonin, only two
returned from the Russian campaign. They were not soldiers.
Most, like Laguipierre, the master chef from the Elysée, had
frozen to death. Napoleon was blamed.

Carême and the Talleyrand household were more aware
than most of the stirrings of change. Aimée de Coigny, one

85

of the old-school of *grandes horizontales*, was mistress by 1812 to the Bourbonist Marquis de Boisgelin. The clatter of her carriage in the *cour d'honneur* above Antonin's kitchen was one sign of the changing winds: Talleyrand, who was already out of favour with Napoleon, was being courted by the supporters of the Bourbon princes in the hope of their return to power. He was playing a dangerous game, and one that could have badly damaged Carême's career. Antonin decided his fortunes might be better served on firmer ground. He started to write a book.

Carême probably first began writing a journal when he was working at Monsieur Bailly's on the rue Vivienne; he undoubtedly made copious notes from the architecture books at the Bibliothèque Nationale. And, by the time he was working, whether at Valençay or in his pâtisserie on the rue de la Paix, he was regularly relieving the tension of his day spent in the kitchen by writing. 'I had the excellent habit,' he said of this period of his life, 'to return each evening *chez moi* and sit, plume in hand...'

The idea of publishing a cookbook was not a great leap from these menu-journals. Most likely Carême had always entertained the possibility of using his notes in this way; the concept of a cookbook was hardly new. Carême had read many in the Bibliothèque Nationale. The chef Varenne's works on pâtisserie and La Chapelle's *La cuisinière moderne* from the previous century had his special praise. But the Revolution had seen a boom in publishing and printing in Paris. One Parisian bookseller, Madame Merigot, sold her potato-obsessed recipes in *La cuisinière républicaine* to the hungry crowds at the Place de la Revolution. The restaurateur Beauvilliers also brought out his own recipe book – beating Antonin into print by a year.

Carême, along with de la Reynière and Brillat-Savarin, wanted to play his part in the 'legislating' of gastronomy, explaining everything in exhaustive detail for the aspirant new bourgeoisie. But his interests were more than culinary, and so was his genius. He hit on a very modern marketing ploy by larding his name and recipes with a sort of fame-by-proximity, suggesting to his publishers they call his first book *Le Pâtissier royal parisien*. In this regard, events beyond his control gave him a key advantage over his rivals.

Alexander I (1777–1825), Tsar of All the Russias, entered Paris at the head of the allied armies ranged against Napoleon in the spring of 1814. The grandson of Catherine the Great, the leader of the victorious allies who had defeated the French at Leipzig, the man who would not sue for peace even as Moscow burned, Alexander was regarded in London and Paris as the very model of a modern monarch. He also loved food rather more than his imperial predecessor, Napoleon. By 1814 this 'Apollo of the North' had a waistline heading south, and used food more and more as a balm for his mystic, tortured self-doubt.

Alexander had much to be tortured about. One bitter St Petersburg night in 1801 his father had been murdered by the Semeonovsky Guards. Alexander had dined with his parents that same evening. The meal had been served, *à la russe*, on porcelain plates depicting views of the Mikhaelovsky prison-palace in which they lived; a palace where it was said every single door was locked at night. Alexander had heard the screams from across the courtyard as the life was crushed from Tsar Paul's throat with one of his own malachite paperweights.

Alexander had known of the plans to depose his father. He may even have known that there was a plan to assassinate him. Chillingly, the day after the murder, Count Pahlen, the chief conspirator, had said to him: 'You cannot make an omelette without breaking eggs.' (The basics of omelette-making would have been news to a previous generation of Russian aristocrats but not to Alexander. His mother, the Empress Maria Feodorovna, had imported many French foods and fashions to the Winter Palace from the court of her friend Marie Antoinette, including occasionally cooking an omelette at table. It was not a practice Alexander's young bride was encouraged to continue.)

When Tsar Alexander entered Paris at the head of the Russian army, he was the first foreign conqueror to ride into the city for 400 years. But the crowds, including Antonin, waved and cheered the man who had 'liberated' them from Napoleon's constant warring. Columns of troops passed down the rue du Faubourg Saint Martin and the rue Royale, turning right above Carême's kitchens on the Place de la Concorde and into the Champs-Elysées. The army later bivouacked under the trees of the Champs-Elysées and around the Arc de Triomphe which Napoleon had commissioned in 1806, but which remained half-built. Only half a day's ride away at Fontainebleau, Bonaparte was on the point of abdicating.

Alexander had still not decided where he should stay in Paris: the Elysée, the Tuileries or elsewhere. Nor was it yet clear who would replace Napoleon. In the meantime, there was a victory parade along the Champs-Elysées, during which the Russian diplomat Karl von Nesselrode received an anonymous note. It was delivered by an unknown member of Talleyrand's household. One story even suggests that Carême – who would have had as much to gain by its delivery as Talleyrand – was the messenger.

The note said that the Elysée Palace had been undermined with gunpowder, and that the Tsar should on no account stay there. It took some days before this was proved to be untrue. Meanwhile, Talleyrand, swiftly dissociating himself from the old regime, offered hospitality at his palace on the rue Saint Florentin. This was accepted by the Tsar.

'Monsieur de Talleyrand,' said the young Tsar in his faultless French, dismounting in the courtyard of the minister's mansion, 'I have decided I shall stay at your home since you possess the confidence of myself and my allies.' A small crowd gathered outside the kitchen windows shouting, 'Hurrah for the Liberators!' and 'Vivat Alexander!' As dusk fell, the Preobrazhensky Grenadiers took their places outside the gates of the Hôtel Talleyrand – for a brief moment, the very epicentre of European politics – and Antonin found himself chef to the most famous and powerful man in the world.

Through the night of 4–5 April 1814, envoys came and went past the imperial bodyguard. Napoleon's emissaries arrived from Fontainebleau, visiting the Tsar on the first floor to argue in favour of a regency for Napoleon's heir, the King of Rome. Below them – and one floor above Antonin's kitchens – Talleyrand received Baron Vitrolles on behalf of the Bourbons. But none of this could keep the Tsar from dinner – as Talleyrand had said, 'We must eat, before we talk.'

In the dining-room of Hôtel Talleyrand, the Tsar found himself in a diplomatic conundrum, one he solved immediately if unconventionally. Expected to toast either the King of Rome, or one of the Bourbon claimants to the French throne, he raised his glass instead to the king of cooks: Carême.

As 3 and then 4am sounded from the bells of the Madeleine, the government of France hung in the balance. 'We must see what happens,' Talleyrand remarked as dawn approached. 'Tsar Alexander does unexpected things – after all he is the son of Paul I.'

At five, the Tsar sent everyone to bed. In the morning, he announced: 'Napoleon must abdicate unconditionally; a regency gives France no prospect of repose,' and ordered breakfast. Napoleon was forced to sign the act of abdication that afternoon, allowing for the restoration of the Bourbon monarchy and the return of Louis XVIII, and by dinner the document was back on the table in the Hôtel Talleyrand. The details – the exile in Elba, the position of Marie Louise of Austria and the little King of Rome – were still to be ironed out, but rarely has the fate of a country lain so clearly in one household and at the dinner table of one man.

As Antonin busied himself with the demands of the new Russian guests, all around Paris the Russian troops were digging in. One regiment, the Semeonovsky Guards, was only narrowly dissuaded from pulling down the Colonne de la Grande Armée in the Place Vendôme, while the Cossacks attempted to steal the statues from the Tuileries Gardens. The French-speaking Russian officers thronged to the *comédies* at the Odéon, while their subordinates, as any Muscovite will proudly boast, insisted that the restaurateurs speed up their service by shouting at them in Russian: '*Bystro, bystro!*' ('Faster, faster!')

When the Tsar eventually moved from the rue Saint Florentin to the Elysée Palace, he was so taken with Carême and his food he asked whether he could borrow the chef for the duration of his stay in Paris. Talleyrand naturally agreed. Carême was kept very busy. Paris was weary of war and, for a 'conqueror' Alexander was surprisingly popular. One of his most chivalrous acts was to pay court to the divorced ex-Empress Joséphine at Malmaison, causing a flurry of excited speculation with Parisian gossips and in the heart of the 50-year-old dowager, who took to wearing flimsy dresses again, caught a chill and died soon after. Everyone seemed delighted by the temporary Romanov regime. Even the radical British writer John Cam Hobhouse was charmed by the sight of the Autocrat of all the Russias waltzing at the Hôtel de Montesquieu.

The ball at the Montesquieu was given by Lord Charles Stewart, the dandified younger brother of the British foreign minister, Lord Castlereagh. Stewart was in return invited by the Tsar to a dinner at the Russian-Elysée. This proved to be a significant evening for Carême, for the meal he prepared was to secure for him, in the future, some of his happiest years of employment. Stewart was part of the new generation of British aristocrats who had read the latest *Manuel des Amphitryons* and Brillat-Savarin's *Physiologie du Goût,* and who prided themselves on their knowledge of food. He was not to forget the dishes he had enjoyed at the Elysée – or the name of their creator.

Back in the kitchens where he had worked under Laguipierre and Riquette, when the palace was known as the Elysée-Napoléon, Carême now found himself with an empire of his own. Much more than a famous pastry chef, he was now *chef de cuisine* in the most important household in Europe. 'My cooking,' he boasted 'was the advance guard of French diplomacy.' For this, he had both Talleyrand's self-serving generosity to thank and the confidence of the comptroller of the Russian household, Muller.

Over those momentous few months in Paris at the Elysée palace, the Russian maitre d' took Antonin aside to assure him that an even greater fortune awaited him if he wanted it, in the Paris of the North: Imperial St Petersburg.

NESSELRODE PUDDING

Carême created this chestnut pudding in honour of the Russian minister in Paris. It subsequently became a favourite of The Prince Regent

Take 40 chestnuts and blanch in boiling water, pound them and add a few spoonfuls of syrup, and then press through a sieve. Mix with a pint of syrup made from one pound of sugar clarified with a stick of vanilla, and place in a bowl with a pint of thick cream and twelve fresh egg yolks. Set this over a gentle heat, and, stirring constantly, take it off just as it is about to boil. Pass through a sieve again. Once cold, add a glass of maraschino brandy. Let set on ice over night. Add an ounce of candied lemon peel, two ounces of currants and two ounces of raisins that have all been soaked overnight in maraschino. Mix, and add another 'plateful' of whipped cream. And three egg whites, stiffly beaten. Set it in a pewter mould and when thus shaped place it in the freezing room covered with ice and saltpetre.

Antonin Carême

CHAPTER 8

The Cook, His Book,
His Wife and His Lover

The universe itself is but a pudding of elements.
Empires, kingdoms, states and republics are but puddings
of people differently made up.

From 'A Learned Dissertation on a Dumpling', an
18th-century pamphlet quoted by Dr William Kitchener
in *The Cook's Oracle* (1817)

Certain 'circumstances', Antonin said, led him to decline the offer of accompanying the Tsar when the Russians eventually left Paris. These circumstances are not so difficult to fathom. For the first time in his life he was publishing a book, and for the first and only time he was going to be a father. This latter fact is less clearly placed.

His daughter, Marie Carême, was of marriageable age by 1832, so she was probably born no later than 1815 – also coincidentally the date of the publication of *Le Pâtissier royal parisien*.

Just before her birth, or as a result of it, it seems, Carême left his wife of the last seven years – or she him – and set up home with the mother of his child, Agathe Guichardet. Agathe was ten years his junior. The fragmentary records of the period may yet reveal more, but it appears that Carême went to some lengths to obliterate the details of what happened, and that something went so awry in his relationship with his only child that she preserved nothing of her father's letters and personal effects.

Meanwhile, the political questions that were debated over Carême's dinners in the Russian-Elysée moved on to Vienna. So, too, did most of Carême's guests. The allies who had defeated Napoleon had set up a peace conference in an attempt to resolve the various territorial issues left in the wake of Bonaparte's demise, as well as the future of France itself. The state of Belgium, the European borders until 1914, the map of Scandinavia and its monarchies all date from this conference – the Congress of Vienna. From November 1814 to June 1815 Vienna became the Continental capital, a 'panorama' as one contemporary put it, of all that was great and good, and not so good, in Europe. Metternich, Talleyrand, Castlereagh, Nesselrode, Charles Stewart, the Duke of Wellington and the Princes Hardenburg and Guillaume de Humboldt, dedicated gourmets all, were in attendance. And Carême? Surprisingly, no (although he is often credited with having been there). At a gathering at which Talleyrand needed more than ever the grease of French cooking on the cogs of his diplomatic machinations, Carême opted to stay away. Instead, he wrote.

Le Pâtissier royal parisien, Antonin's first book, was published in September 1815. Two, heavy, 400-page volumes describe flamboyant *extraordinaires* and simple puddings. Its recipes, many carefully illustrated by Carême, are still the staples of modern French pâtisserie: *babas* and *madeleines*, flans and *pithiviers*; Chantilly creams, fruit jellies, fromage bavarois, ice creams and blancmanges. *Le Pâtissier* was such a success that a second edition came out in December, with the short sections on cold collations removed and various additions made in response to those who had criticised the first edition: 'Maybe my style does not please,' wrote Antonin, 'it is uncorrected, that much is true, but it is the style of a working man, an artisan… My drawings you say lack aplomb; this is very possible. I was never taught to draw; they are there as illustration to my art.' He took drawing lessons before publishing his next book.

The advice on meals and eating in *Le Pâtissier royal parisien* is as relevant today as it was for the hosts of the intimate dinner parties catered for by Carême. 'A small dinner party meal should last as little as two hours but ideally three or more,' says Antonin. 'Overloading the table is a great crime. Our menu, supposing six or eight reasonable eaters, would be complete with six elaborate and substantial plates.' Carême advised that food should be served on hot plates, and insisted on strict hygiene. He also recommended using seasonal produce. He favoured seafood for these less grandiose evenings: turbot, salmon, lobsters from Cherbourg, shrimps from Honfleur. 'Salmon and turbot,' he said, 'must be lightly cooked and served with their own juices and sauces made from old wines to help the digestive action of the stomach.' Heavier meats, he was convinced, should be left for more 'princely' occasions.

Carême also began to form theories about the marriage of fine wine and food. He suggested sherry after a light first course, or with the soup course to inspire the appetite; he approved of Talleyrand's habit of drinking watered-down Madeira with meals; and suggested the liberal use of champagne with food and within recipes. Dessert, Carême suggested, was the reward at the end of the meal – especially 'for young ladies and children at table', and sherry again appears with 'old cheeses' – seemingly, in the manner now described as 'English': that is, between dessert and coffee. Carême advised coffee to be served at table – his admirer the Marquis de Cussy complained that his had 'always been cold in the salon'. The practices of dining, like so much at the time, were changing.

The title Carême chose for his book allied him with the restored monarchy, but he also describes Napoleonic banquets and dedicates the work neither to king nor emperor nor even to Talleyrand, but to plain Monsieur Boucher, the man who had first given him his big break when he 'discovered' him at Bailly's pâtisserie.

Paris was quieter than normal through the winter and spring of 1814–15 – *le beau monde* were all in Vienna. Such peace, however, was shattered by the news that reached the Congress on 7 March 1815 and Antonin in Paris the next day: Napoleon had escaped from his imprisonment on Elba. The pace of events was dazzling. Napoleon's followers numbered only 750 when he escaped his island prison in late February. By May he had more than quarter of a million. Louis XVIII fled Paris, Napoleon met his Waterloo, and by late July 1815 Tsar Alexander was back in the Elysée. '*Quelle affaire!*' as Marshal Blücher famously remarked to Wellington.

From 1 August to 26 September 1815 Carême, too, was back in charge of the kitchens at the Russian-Elysée at the centre of European affairs – now taking careful note of every menu served, for future publication. What follows is the first meal Tsar Alexander ate on his return to Paris after the second fall of Napoleon. The service was divisible by three in every case, so that one part could go to the imperial table, and two parts to the larger table of generals.

MENU

Served to Tsar Alexander à la russe
at the Elysée Palace 1st August 1815

12 places at His Imperial Majesty's table
24 places at the table for the princes and generals
36 covers in total

36 plates of oysters, 24 lemons

THREE SOUPS

Cold Russian soup

Consommé with quenelles à l'Allemande

Potage Condé

౿

THREE PLATES OF HORS D'OEUVRES

Pear-shaped game croquettes

౿

THREE PLATES OF COLD ENTRÉES

Salmon steaks au beurre Montpellier

౿

THREE GROSSES PIÈCES

Beef à la Flamande

౿

NINE HOT ENTRÉES

Three chicken à l'ivoire with a herb sauce

Three partridge à la maréchal, sauce financier

Three veal brains glacé à la Macédoine

౿

THREE PLATES OF ROASTS WITH SALAD

Roast chicken, loin of veal

౿

SIX VEGETABLE ENTREMETS

French peas
Artichokes à la Lyonnaise

NINE DESSERTS

Vanilla soufflés
Orange meringues
Mocha coffee mousses

Access to provisions – artichokes, oranges, fresh veal brains – was clearly not a problem for Carême during the continued turmoil in and around the French capital. But the mood in Paris was brittle. An angry crowd met British troops deputised to remove Italian treasures from the Louvre for repatriation, and everywhere there was uncertainty over the 'White (Bourbon) Terror' that might exact vengeance on the Bonapartistes.

Antonin felt safe enough in the kitchens of the Elysée. The Tsar was now said to be a virtual recluse compared with the dashing figure he had cut the year before. He ate, very well, but only with his generals. One reason for this was the new love in his life, a widowed mystic called Julie Von Krudener. Some gossips rumoured that the grey-haired matron secretly met the Tsar by way of the Elysée gardens and kitchens. Antonin, if he was aware of any intruder, held his tongue on the matter. Yet the cook and the baroness did meet. By coincidence, Madame Von Krudener was to reach the apotheosis of her bizarre career in France at the same time and place as Carême: in a field in Champagne called Vertus.

The allies felt the need of some ceremony to mark the final departure of the Tsar for his homeland. The day chosen for the victory festival was the feast-day, 11 September, of Tsar Alexander's patron, Saint Alexander Nevsky, at whose shrine on Nevsky Prospect in St Petersburg departing soldiers still pray. Carême was contracted to cater, and an open-air venue was chosen near Épernay in Champagne.

For one thing, this was the site of the desperate last 'victory' of Napoleon, gained with the pitchforks of the people of Épernay, and fuelled by free champagne from their mayor, Jean Moët. For another, no Paris venue was large enough for the intended cast. An open-air thanksgiving High Mass was planned, as well as a march-past, with more than 150 squadrons of cavalry, 150 battalions of infantry and 900 officers. The Tsar would attend with Emperor Francis of Austria, King Frederick William of Prussia, Prince Schwarzenberg, Marshal Blücher and the Duke of Wellington – and Madame Von Krudener, who, in her habitual blue serge dress and straw hat, must have appeared an unlikely figure among all the braid and medals.

The Plein de Vertus is some 80 miles to the east of Paris, between Montmirail, Chalons and Épernay, in a sort of natural amphitheatre. As a Champs-de-Mars the location had some advantages, but, for the caterer – Carême – it could hardly have been more problematic. Carême was asked to provide three formal feasts – on the nights of 10, 11 and 12 September – for 300 guests each, as well as smaller formal meals for the royal parties.

A butcher had arrived from Paris some days earlier with a herd of cattle, veal calves and a flock of sheep, and set up an abattoir. Letters went back and forth to the Mayor of Chalons in search of local ice as the Paris ice-mongers were demanding 50 centimes a pound to take ice blocks to Vertus. Eventually an entire ice house was bought locally. Next came Antonin himself, at the head of 40 chefs, wagons carrying tables for 300 covers, 200 pieces of cooking equipment, linen, wine, fowl, vegetables, flour, sugar, eggs – and King Louis's own architect, Fontaine, to decorate the marquees and tables. After a journey on which they nervously eyed the Cossack troops who lined the route, Antonin and the chefs set up camp just outside Chalons. They slept, to Antonin's eternal chagrin, on the straw-strewn floor of a barn.

The Russian engineer Baron de Sarth had requisitioned peasants from 13 villages to flatten the hilltop and erect balustrades and viewing platforms for the expected crowds. Russian troops massed in Vertus all through August, and Alexander sent memos to his generals and his chef alike, checking every detail 20 times per day and studying Fontaine's drawings to determine that this, the anniversary of his coronation, should be Russia's greatest day in France. And so it turned out to be, according to the Russian writer Danilevsky, the essayist Sydney Smith, the Iron Duke Wellington and Carême himself.

The initial march past involved seven horse and 11 infantry divisions, three Cossack regiments with 540 field guns, a total of 150,000 soldiers including 3,980 chief officers in full regalia. Lord Charles Stewart wrote to his elder brother Viscount Castlereagh: 'On the arrival of the sovereigns at the spot fixed for them, the ensign was unfurled. The whole Russian army was seen drawn up in three lines, extending as far as the eye could reach. The sun glittered on their arms and on the drawn sabres of the cavalry, to a distance that almost appeared imaginary... along which the cavalcade of monarchs and their immense suite rode.'

The troops and monarchs next arranged themselves, in a square that extended to the horizon, around seven altars – the mystic number of the Apocalypse – while Orthodox priests celebrated High Mass according to the Russian liturgy. The Tsar toured the altars with the spiritualist Von Krudener keening at his side.

'My heart was filled with love of my enemies,' he wrote, 'and I prayed that France might be saved.'

'Well, Charles,' Wellington turned to Lord Stewart and whispered, 'you and I never saw such a sight before and never shall again.'

Next, the monarchs, generals, officers and ladies repaired to Carême's dinner. Fontaine and Carême had designed 42 Gothic pavilions to house the banquet, with similarly chivalric-themed table decorations, all at the foot of the ruined château of Mont-Amie. There were smaller pavilions in the 'garden' of the Tsar's tent. The scene, said to look like a dream out of a Walter Scott novel, was recorded by Pazetti, the court painter from The Hermitage, as if to prove that the Russians could teach the French something about glamorous banqueting.

Carême, patriotically, chose to serve dinner *à la française*. First the guests were given fresh oysters – 300 plates with 150 lemons – followed by three soups. Next were 28 different hors d'oeuvres, cold entrées, sides of beef in Madeira, followed by 112 hot entrées, as well as plates of cut roasts, salads, side-dishes of vegetables and desserts. 'It seemed,' wrote Lady Edgcumbe, 'more like a tale in the *Arabian Nights* than an occurrence in real life.'

VERTUS BANQUET

11th September 1815

300 plates of oysters, 150 lemons

THREE SOUPS

150 Potage à la Russe
150 Potage à la Reine
150 Julienne au blond de veau

28 PLATES HORS D'OEUVRES

Croustades à la béchamel

28 PLATES COLD ENTRÉES

Jellied chicken mayonnaise

28 GROSSES PIÈCES

Beef à la Macédoine in Madeira

112 HOT ENTRÉES

Filet de turbot, anchovy butter sauce

Veal heads in a turtle Madeira sauce

Chicken fricassée à la Chevalier

Vols-au-vents à la Toulouse

28 PLATES OF ROASTS AND SALAD

Quails, chicken, loin of veal

56 VEGETABLE ENTREMETS

Artichokes à la Lyonnaise

French peas

56 DESSERTS

Meringues stuffed with vanilla cream
Verjuice jellies moulded with fruit cooked in Madeira
8 extra plates of fondues for the table of the Emperor

Local legend tells that children collected oyster shells in a Champagne field for generations to come. Yet Antonin, somewhere in his heart forever a lost boy, remembered his day of triumph as much for the bitter ignominy of again sleeping rough, in a hay barn.

He returned to Paris to carry on cooking at the Elysée and recorded menus up to 28 September. Then Alexander, Muller and the Russian army departed for St Petersburg. Julie Von Krudener's dream of a Holy Alliance 'to take as its sole guide the precepts of the Christian religion' was more or less in place.

Through the winter of 1815 to 1816 Antonin became even more associated with the restored Bourbon throne than his bestselling *Le Pâtissier royal* might suggest. He brought out a companion book, *Le Pâtissier pittoresque*, which concentrated on his celebrated royal *extraordinaires*, and he created more of these for the Bourbon Count d'Artois and the Duchesse de Berry. In February 1816, he took on a series of commissions that formed the centrepieces at key occasions of Bourbon propaganda.

The army was still split in 1816, in spirit if not in practice, between the royalist and the (formerly) Bonapartiste factions. But on 5 February, in a gesture of reconciliation, the Garde Royale and the Royal Garde du Corps gave a ball and dinner in the Grande Galerie of the Louvre in honour of the formerly Bonapartiste Garde Nationale. The restored King Louis XVIII was to be guest of honour.

The man in charge of the catering was the restaurateur Heneveu, who had become rich on the proceeds of the private romantic boudoirs he had cannily installed at his rue du Temple restaurant. Over 100 chefs were involved in the affair, with Antonin concentrating on the sugarwork and cold entrées. A new oven, 50 foot by six foot, was built for the occasion, and a separate newly restored palace room allocated to the famous Palladio of Pastry.

Twelve hundred covers were laid on 12 tables, each table celebrating a famous military hero. Carême made *extraordinaires* in his favourite style of the period – giant military trophies – in sugar and mastic, up to two metres high, one for each table. 'In the middle of the gallery,' he wrote, 'a grand orchestra played familiar airs and a salvo of artillery-fire

> Pièce montée – *a stuffed boar's head. Carême's* savoury *pièces* montées *were invariably shot through with numerous* hâtelets, *or skewers, so that an array of delicacies could be picked off easily by guests*

announced the entry of King Louis XVIII from his Louvre apartments… Ah!' gushed Antonin, 'despite our recent troubles, what nation on earth could mount to an astonished universe such an august reunion! I was proud to be French.'

However, things were not quite as august below stairs. Tempers flared in the heat of the neglected Louvre kitchens. Heneveu had provided the wrong fish for one recipe, and Carême's charlottes flopped when they were mishandled on to their plates. It can happen to the best of chefs. Yet Antonin insisted that there was malign intent on the part of some of the other, jealous, chefs of Paris.

On 21 February, the Garde Nationale issued a return invitation to the royal regiments, this time to a dinner for 3,000 in the glamorous setting of the Odéon theatre. Carême again was contracted, this time by the restaurateur Bertrand, to cook in the kitchens of the Petit Luxembourg palace with a Monsieur Arlet and then transport the *extraordinaires* by tumbrels the short distance along the road to l'Odéon.

Carême designed a buffet in the French style with nine tiers of food, which stood in the lobby of the theatre. There were 90 Portuguese hams, galantines of turkey perched on top of pedestals dressed with fish, and 160 plates with selections of eight prepared foods, for instance partridge salmis in aspic. There were also 90 huge pâtisseries, both sweet and savoury, stuffed with cold game pâtés or decorated with spun sugar, 250 plates of roast meats each made up of 25 larded quails, partridge and chicken *à la reine* with roast ducklings in Seville orange sauce. There were even 200 *entremets*: crowns of crayfish, little pots of blancmange (not sweet then, but a savoury mousse) and Maraschino jellies. There were 600 dessert plates, chestnut mousses, vanilla *fromages*, and 100 cakes iced to look like military drums. Just to pick at, there were 3,000 *petit pains*. And to drink: over 3,000 bottles of wine.

'The Odéon looked dazzlingly beautiful,' wrote Antonin, 'in the light of a thousand candles, the front-of-house columns all draped in cloth of gold and silver and each crowned with an immense wreath of flowers and the legend *Happy Times! Louis Returns!* The principal box hosted the royal family, the next boxes the ladies of the court, then the dukes and peers, then the deputies and ministers, the ambassadors and the marshals. The rest of the boxes were garnished with ladies each rivalling the next in beauty and jewels. At this ball shone all the elegance and all the gaiety that distinguishes our manners.'

But if this extravagantly theatrical evening looked like 'the epitome of French elegance', it also proved again the difficulty of *service à la française*. Carême's nine tiers of food could not easily be accessed by the '*chevaliers*', who went back

Next page: A tiered buffet of the style created in the foyer of the Odéon theatre. This illustration, so large it had to be published as a 'pull-out' at the end of Maître d'hôtel *in 1822, was drawn by Carême himself, perhaps to illustrate the problem of displays that were more dramatic than serviceable*

and forth to the boxes to serve their ladies, and there were many complaints. 'The essential thing,' Carême realised, 'even at these enormous parties must be the satisfaction of *all* the guests.'

As spring moved into summer in 1816 and Louis XVIII's famous girth expanded in accordance with the style in which he sought to win over Paris, Carême began to tire of '*le gigantisme culinaire*'. Nevertheless, he agreed to participate in a dinner for 10,000 veterans on the Champs-Elysées – a spectacular example of tactical Bourbon munificence in a reign typified by extravagant entertaining.

From the Place de la Concorde – or Place Louis XV as Antonin insisted on still calling it – to the edge of Étoile and its still incomplete Arc de Triomphe, a long tent was erected. On either side of this tented corridor, two tables stretched the length of the avenue, under the young trees, decked with 10,000 bottles of wine. One bottle for each guest – just to start. Six whole oxen were roasted, 75 veal calves, 250 lambs, along with 2,000 chickens, 8,000 turkeys, 500 hams and tongues and over 2,000 carp, pike and partridges.

There were 1,000 pâtés, 1,000 biscuits and *babas*, and, as dinner progressed, another 18,000 bottles of Macon rouge were consumed. A selection of the food, as well as 145 carafes of wine, were given to the then 12 arrondissements of Paris in imitation of the practice of medieval kings. Carême toiled with Monsieur Lasne and many others at the kitchens of the Hôtel de Ville. A great day in the history of food in Paris, but, wrote Carême, 'never had work been so hellish for the chefs.'

A timely proposal awaited him when he returned home: a letter of introduction from the court of the Prince Regent of England – and the prospect of an easier life across the Channel.

ORANGE-FLOWER AND PINK
CHAMPAGNE JELLY

Boil 12 ounces of sugar in enough water to cover, add the orange flowers and remove from the heat. Allow to infuse, and strain, cold, through silk. Add one ounce and two drams of isinglass and mix this and the strained syrup* into a bottle of pink champagne, previously opened. The juice of a lemon may be added, and a drop of cochineal if the colour seems weak without it; tiny drops of the dye, slightly dried out before the jelly is added, will set in a marbled effect. Set in glasses or mould with orange blossom.

Antonin Carême

---

* orange flower water and gelatine may substitute.

CHAPTER 9

The Brighton Pavilion

Who's your fat friend?

Beau Brummell to the man accompanying the Prince Regent

George, Prince of Wales (1762–1830), created Regent in 1811 after the final descent into madness of his father George III, adored all things French. The lavish interiors of Carlton House (his palace in London on Pall Mall) were decorated in the French neoclassical style and filled with French furniture. He had a morbid fascination with the executed family of Louis XVI and collected their portraits in miniature. In later life, the Regent became obsessed with the tiny figure of Napoleon, collecting art and artefacts connected with the vanquished Emperor, as well as anecdotes from those who – like Carême – had been associated with him. Above all, the Prince Regent loved French food. When his brother, the Duke of Cambridge, visited Paris and wrote to the Regent that 'It is impossible to live better!', George replied that the 'gourmet king' Louis XVIII of France 'need not find my table in any way inferior to his own' – and he set about recruiting a French chef to prove it.

The Clerk Comptroller of his household, Jean Baptiste Watier, was sent to Paris in search of such a man. In his wildest dreams the Prince Regent can hardly have expected that Watier would return with quite the catch he did. Watier had first approached the Parisian chefs Messieurs Robert and Lasne with a view to finding someone *associated* with Carême. He never expected that Carême himself – who, after the meals he had prepared for the Tsar, was now talked about as 'the best cook in the world' – would agree to come to England almost immediately. But he did.

Carême later claimed that he had made this decision because the Prince Regent promised him £2,000 a year. This is an astonishing figure when one considers that the Prince had caused a small scandal in the past by employing a chef for what was then regarded as the vast sum of £200 a year, when he was in any case £390,000 in debt. Carême was being offered twice the pay of Lord Cholmondeley, the Lord Steward, three times more than the Clerk Comptroller who had made the offer, or, in today's money, an annual salary of over £250,000.

Carême left for England in July 1816, leaving Agathe and little Marie in Paris. In the absence of any word from him on the subject of why he left so hastily without his family, his motives must remain a matter of speculation. He may simply have wanted the money. However the timing and alacrity of his departure beg questions over the state of his relationship with Agathe – and by extension little Marie – as it seems likely that they never lived together again as man and wife. To judge by Marie's later bitterness about her father, Antonin abandoned this second 'marriage' only a few years after it had begun.

His work in London and Brighton took Carême out of France for the first time. He had no need to learn English: half the Regent's below stairs staff were French or French-speaking Germans. There were even five French clergy in the Regent's household. And extra French footmen were hired for Carême's arrival – the young Messieurs Lucas, Dupasguire and Jaccard. Always right-handed, these footmen were paid – eccentrically to the modern mind but in the contemporary fashion of *corps de ballets* – according to their height: tall footmen made more elegant servers, negotiating with their hot *assiettes volantes* the plumed headdresses of the ladies. So Antonin was surrounded in England by his countrymen – even if many of them would have looked down on him.

By the time Carême met the Prince Regent, the prince's love of all things French had expanded his weight to 20 stone and his waist to 50 inches, so that his belly, when uncorseted from its 'Bastille of Whalebone', reached his knees. Antonin told the Prince that the 'purity' of his cooking would alleviate his periods of chronic pain (thought now to be symptoms of the porphyria from which his father suffered) and even reduce his weight. It was an idle boast. The medical records and letters of the Prince during 1816 and 1817 show that he was as poorly as ever – suffering from 'colic', acute gout and recurrent 'lassitude' – and that, if anything, he put on weight during Antonin's reign over his kitchens. The Prince Regent once teased Carême that the temptations of his cooking would be the death of him. 'Your Highness,' replied Carême, 'my concern is to tempt your appetite; yours is to curb it.'

At Brighton and Carlton House, Carême found at his disposal the best produce money and advantage could purchase. The surviving kitchen accounts reveal that the Royal Gardens at Kensington supplied most of his needs. In one month in 1817, for example, the kitchens took supply of 153 dozen sprouting broccoli, 428 bunches of radishes, 118 dozen Savoy cabbages, nearly a dozen bunches of asparagus made up of 100 heads each, 63 dozen seakale (new to Carême), 7 dozen Cos lettuces which he used often, steamed, as a garnish, and most of which would have had to have been grown under glass. Between 5 June and 7 July 1816, the gardens at Kensington produced 117 large baskets of strawberries and 160 more came from Hampton and Kew. Hothouse peaches, nectarines, grapes, cherries, figs, raspberries, melons and the admired pineapple were also grown.

A single month's expenditure on meat is even more startling: £258 12 shillings and 3 farthings was spent on 1,854 pounds of beef, 1,625 pounds of mutton and 1,785 pounds of veal. The poultry bill for the same month came to £323 5 shillings and 6 pence – for 385 pullets, 232 chickens, 88 quails, 31 capons, 12 geese and 10 rabbits. Also on the menu: 118 pounds of 'old' ham and 262 pounds of fresh ham – and 61 lobsters. In April 1817, after a severe winter, Carême apologised for the limited variety of his menus – only four or five fruit or vegetable options in meals of 30 different dishes!

Carême cooked first for the 'Prince of Whales' at Carlton House in London. Now lost, save for a few pillars on the National Gallery, Carlton House could have been designed to please the Parisian confectioner. 'Not a spot without some paint upon it – gold upon gold,' said the artist Farington. Carême adored the sense of theatre and spectacle that dominated the experience of dining there. His love of wild Gothic embellishment and chinoiserie themes was perfectly reflected in the décor and table-settings. But, like one of Carême's *extraordinaires*, nothing was ever quite what it seemed.

Facings were used to disguise the real nature of what lay beneath; Gothic arches were made of iron; veneers of coloured marble covered the walls; swans were made of bronze; and bronze was imitated in paint. The grand entrance at street level off Pall Mall, similarly, disguised the fact that there was an enormous 'below stairs' area hidden on the sloping ground to the south. Carême found here, half underground, the largest kitchens in London, with separate confectionery and pastry rooms, and an entire room devoted to the Prince's silver plate.

The most eccentric architectural 'folly' of Carlton House was the Gothic conservatory, linked to the dining-room, where Antonin's banquets were served. A reinvention of Westminster Abbey's nave in coloured glass and iron, it was then the largest glasswork building in the world. Antonin 'gasped' when he first saw this 'Mahomet's Paradise'. 'All the details are gold on white,' he wrote, 'setting off the stained-glass windows. The crystal chandeliers, the ornaments and furniture, everything recalls the most luxurious Asiatic taste; the buffet all dressed in cold meat... posed on gold and silver.'

There was room for a 200-foot-long table, the longest in London, which could be embellished with a flowing rivulet of water, springing from a silver fountain at the head of the table. The stream, the centrepiece, was dressed with real moss and flowers and sported real – or, on occasion, gold – goldfish. Four silver bridges served as table decorations, one with a small tower on it. It was all 'as if in masquerade', according to one guest, 'full of jars and mandarins and pagodas... They sleep in Turkish tents and dine in a Gothic chapel.'

But, as things turned out, Carême rarely cooked for the 'cathedral dining-room' at Carlton House, the only major banquet being for the visit of the Archduke Nicholas of Russia in early 1817. By then, the spendthrift Prince had become so unpopular in London that he was pelted with stones en route to the State Opening of Parliament and 'Bread or the Regent's Head!' was daubed on the walls of Carlton House just above Carême's new kitchens. The Prince – and his chef – found it politic to decamp to Brighton.

The Royal Pavilion at Brighton had always been a cook's palace – in fact, the site was originally chosen by the Prince's ex-chef Louis Weltje. The pastry kitchens and ice rooms (now demolished) occupied a quarter of the entire acreage of the palace. The Prince, after all, was there to eat much more than to take the sea cure.

When Carême first saw the palace in the summer of 1816, John Nash's redevelopment of the original pavilion (designed by Henry Holland) into the Orientalist fantasy that exists today was only half-complete. But the kitchens were ready: they had been hastily completed in time for his arrival. If Antonin gasped when he first saw the dining-rooms of Carlton House, nothing could have prepared him for the splendour of his new kitchens at Brighton. Adjacent to, and on the same level as the dining-room, they were a source of wonder to visitors and formed part of the tour for the Prince's guests.

The Comtesse de Boigne, who was in Brighton at the same time as Carême, noted that the 'special point [of the Pavilion was] the kitchens... entirely steam-heated by a system at that time new'. And a reporter from *The Brighton Ambulator* gushed that 'in the furnishing of the kitchen... every modern improvement to facilitate the process of the culinary art has been introduced in all its boasted perfection. It is not exceeding the faithful observation of a narrator in stating that the regency [kitchens] form one part of the most useful and convenient appendages to a mansion that is to be seen in the British Empire.'

Next page: The Royal Pavilion at Brighton, where the pastry kitchens and ice rooms occupied a quarter of the entire acreage. The Great Kitchen itself was hurriedly completed for Carême's arrival.

Twelve remote-controlled sash windows in the roof above the 1,600 square-foot kitchen bathed Antonin's working day in light. Copper wall lamps with tin reflectors and four hexagonal lanterns fitted with Argand oil lamps lit the room at night.

There were bottle-jacks to turn the roasting spits by clock-work; larger joints were turned by smoke-jacks powered by the flue of the fire itself. And in the centre of the room was the pièce de résistance, a 13-foot-long oval steam table which could keep dozens of dishes hot for simultaneous serving.

At Valençay, the Elysée palace, let alone the field at Vertus, the problem of serving elaborate hot menus *à la française* must have created a nightmare of last-minute reheatings and rearrangements. At Brighton, however, Carême boasted that his new steam table could keep 40 presentation platters heated at once. It is depicted in *Nash's Views of the Royal Pavilion* being used to warm six roasts and dozens of smaller dishes under giant cloches. The metal tabletop was heated from underneath with steam from 'a very large strong copper boiler' located behind the kitchen range. The condensed steam ran off eventually into drains, and with its 'multiplicity of conducting pipes' the table was considered 'an admirable specimen of mechanical invention'.

Further kitchen equipment worth £6,000 was ordered for Carême's arrival from William Stark, a local blacksmith and engineer: copper awnings over the ranges decorated with copper ornaments; and three hot closets at three of the corners of the great room and a matching linen cupboard, all fitted with copper shelves and folding doors lined with tinplate. A colossal *batterie de cuisine*, each pan individually engraved by Stark with its shelf number, was arranged on large dressers on the east and west walls so that Carême could see at a glance what was ready for use – or broken. One of the chef's duties was to sign for breakages and repairs.

Beyond the great kitchen itself, there were two pastry and three confectionery rooms, a smaller steam kitchen and larders, all interconnected around a courtyard within yards of the 'decking room' where the majority of dishes that did not need to be kept hot were dressed for the dining-room next door. A water tower in the centre of the courtyard sent hot and cold running water gushing to all areas of the kitchens.

Carême had some say in the final stages of the design, including the provision of additional lead-lined ice bins near his precious confectionery rooms. By chance the Prince Regent had created 'the most fantastic palace in Europe' on land ideally suited for Carême's craft: ice houses were at their most efficient when built above chalk soils. The Brighton Pavilion's giant straw-insulated ice house had sufficient capacity to rent out space to Brighton's ice-mongers and still have surplus ice for sale to local confectioners.

Much of this 'below stairs' pavilion known to Carême has since disappeared: the ice house, water tower and pastry rooms, completed in his time, and even the famous oval table are no more. The blue Dutch tiles familiar to Antonin still line the servants' hallway behind the kitchens, but the network of larders, offices and servants' rooms has now been replaced by modern buildings and where Antonin once lived there is a high-street bank.

Surviving in all its multicoloured exuberance, however, is the dining-room with its ton-weight crystal chandelier dangling from the claws of a dragon flying over the dinner table. Antonin excitedly watched the dining-room's completion during breaks from the kitchen: it was exactly the sort of design that he had adored since his adolescent studies in the Bibliothèque Nationale.

The first meals served in the dining-room, before the paint was even dry on the ceiling's foliage, were probably the dinners, created in honour of the visit of Tsar Alexander's brother, Archduke Nicholas, and served on the nights of the 14, 16 and 18 January 1817. The following menu, served on the guests' last night in Brighton, is only slightly more elaborate than the two menus that preceded it:

DINNER SERVED IN THE BRIGHTON PAVILION TO HRH THE PRINCE REGENT and GRAND DUKE NICHOLAS OF RUSSIA

18th January 1817

EIGHT SOUPS

Les profitralles de volaille à la moderne

Le potage santé au consommé

Le potage de mouton à l'Anglaise

Le potage de riz à la Crécy

Le potage de pigeons à la marinière

Le potage de karick à l'Indienne

Le potage à l'Orléans

Le potage de céleri, consommé de volaille

EIGHT RELEVÉS DE POISSON

Les perches à la Hollandaise

La truite saumonée à la Génoise

Le cabillaud à la crème

Le brocket à l'Espagnol garni de laitances

Les soles au gratin et aux truffes

Le turbot, sauce aux crevettes

Les merlans frits à l'Anglaise

La hure d'esturgeon au vin de Champagne

FIFTEEN ASSIETTES VOLANTES
À SERVIR APRÈS LES POISSONS

De petits vol-au-vents à la Reine

De petit pâtés de mauviettes

De croquettes à la royale

De canetons à la Luxembourg

De filets de poissons à l'Orly

EIGHT GROSSES PIÈCES

Le quartier de sanglier marine

Les poulardes à l'Anglaise

Les filets de bœuf à la Napolitaine

Les faisans truffés à la Perigueux

La dinde à la Godard moderne

La longe de veau à la Monglas

Les perdrix aux choux et racines glacés

Le rosbif de quartier de mouton

FORTY ENTRÉES

(arranged around the relevés de poissons as indicated)

Le sante de poulardes à la d'Artois

Les ris de veau glacés à la chicorée

La croustade de grives au gratin

Charles Maurice de Talleyrand-Périgord
(1754–1838): 'God gave you the choice between
snake and tiger and you chose to be an anaconda'

Napoleon I (1769–1921): 'You must enetertain in
my stead,' he told Talleyrand. 'Only if you want
to eat quickly chez moi'

LA FAMILLE IMPÉRIALE

Napleon's extended family, for whom the term
nouveau-riche was invented, were given titles,
lands and lessons in etiquette

The Prince Regent (1762–1830): 'My concern is to tempt your appetite, Your Highness, yours is to curb it'

The Great Kitchen of the Royal Pavilion,
Brighton. The palm fronds were added after
Carême's departure, but the kitchen was
otherwise as Carême would have known it; a
rare example from the period of below-stairs life

The Banqueting room of the Royal Pavilion,
Brighton. This was still incomplete when
Carême returned to France, but nevertheless
he applauded its chinoiserie style

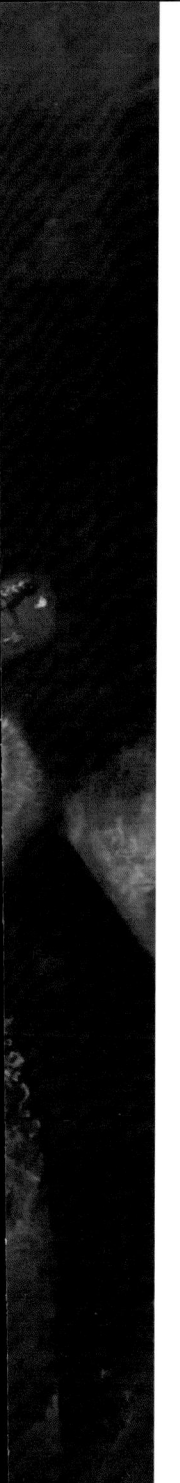

Charles Stewart, the 'Golden Pheasant' of the
Congress of Vienna (1778–1854)

Pavlovsk Palace was a gift of Catherine the Great
to her son Paul and his wife Marie Feodorovna.
Designed by the Scottish architect Cameron, it
was a temple to imported French style. On the
day Caroline arrived in 1819, the local schoolboys
lined the approach road to cheer; one of them
was Alexander Pushkin

Carême missed the Cornotation of George IV
in 1821 and the accompanying banquets. 'I was
happy not to have been there,' Carême wrote,
'from what I heard it was the saddest, shabbiest
affair which my former colleagues from Carlton
House had utterly miscarried'

Betty de Rothschild (1805–1886), painted by her
friend Ingres, married her uncle James in 1823

Les poulets à la reine, à la Chevry

Les côtelettes de lapereaux en lorgnette

(Les perches à la Hollandaise)

Les quenelles de volaille en turban

Les cailles à la mirepoix, ragoût à la financière

La magnonaise de perdreaux à la gelée

L'emince de langues à la Clermont

Les poulets dépéces à l'Italienne

(La truite saumonée à la Génoise)

Les filets de volaille en demi-deuil

Les aiguillettes de canards à la bigarade

La darne de saumon au beurre de Montpellier

Le pain de volaille à la royale

Les filets d'agneaux à la Toulouse

(Le cabillaud à la crème)

La caisse de lapereaux au laurier

La blanquette de poulardes aux champignons

La casserole au riz à la Monglas

Les petits canetons à la Nivernoise

Le sauté de faisans à la Perigord

Les sautés de perdreaux au suprême

La chevalier de poulets garni d'Orly

La timbale de nouilles à la Polonaise

Les escalopes de chevreuil à l'Espagnole

Les ballotines de poulardes à la tomate

(Les soles au gratin)

Les bécasses, entrée de broche à l'Espagnole

Les filets de volaille à la belle vue

Les hâtelets d'aspic de filets de soles

Les cervelles de veaux à la Milanaise

Les escalopes de gelinottes, sauce salmis

(Le turbot, sauce aux crevettes)

Les filets de poulardes glacés aux concombres

Les boudins de faisins à la Richelieu

La salade de volaille à l'ancienne

La noix de jambon aux épinards

Les ailerons de poulardes à la Piémontaise

(Les merlans frits à l'Anglaise)

Les pigeons au beurre d'écrevisses

La poularde à la Maquignon

Le vol-au-vent à la Nesle, Allemande

Les côtelettes de moutons à la purée de pommes de terres

Les filets de poulardes à la Pompadour

EIGHT PIÈCES MONTÉES

An Italian pavilion

A Swiss hermitage

Giant Parisian meringue

Croque-en-bouche aux pistache

A Welsh hermitage

A grand pavilion (the Brighton Pavilion in pastry)

Un gros nougat à la français

Croque-en-bouche aux anis

EIGHT ROASTS

Les bécasses bardées

Le dindonneau

Les faisans piqués

Les poulardes au cresson

Les sarcelles au citron

Les poulets à la reine

Les gelinottes

Les cailles bardées

THIRTY-TWO ENTREMETS

(of which 16 are desserts, with indication of
arrangement around roasts and grosses pièces)

Les concombres farcies au velouté

La gelée de groseilles (conserve)

(Les bécasses bardées)

Les gaufres aux raisins de Corinthe

Les épinards à l'Anglaise

(Le Pavilion Italian)

Le buisson des homards

Les tartelettes d'abricots pralinées

(Les dindonneaux)

La gelée de marasquins fouettée

Les œufs brouilles aux truffes

(La grosse meringue à la Parisienne)

Les navets à la Chartres

Le pouding de pommes au rhum

(Les faisans piques)

Les diadèmes au gros sucré

Les choux-fleurs à la magnonaise

(L'Hermitage Suisse)

Les truffes à la serviette

Les fanchonettes aux avelines

(Les poulardes au cressons)

La gelée de citrons renversées

La croûte aux champignons

Les cardes à l'Espagnol

La gelée de fraises (conserve)

(Les cailles bardées)

Les gâteaux renversés, glacés au gros sucré

Le buisson de crevettes

(Le Pavilion Asiatique)

La salade de salsifis à l'Italienne

Les gâteaux à la dauphine

(Les gelinottes)

134

Le fromage Bavarois aux abricots

Les laitues à l'essence de jambon

(Le nougat à la Française)

Les champignons grilles demi-glacé

Les pannequets à la Chantilly

(Les poulets à la reine)

Les pains à la Duchesse

Les truffes à la serviette

(L'Hermitage Gaulois)

Les pommes de terre à la Lyonnaise

Les gâteaux d'amandes glaces à la rose

(Les sarcelles aux citrons)

La gelée de cuirassau de Hollande

Les céleris à l'Espagnol

TWELVE ASSIETTES VOLANTES

4 soufflés de pomme

4 soufflés à la vanille

4 fondus

This extraordinarily lavish meal laid on by the Prince Regent
– and Carême – for the delectation of the Russians was not
there just to be eaten. Indeed no one – not even the gluttonous

Prince Regent – could have sampled more than a fraction of the whole. As Antonin remarked, 'The man who calls himself a gourmand but eats like a glutton is not a gourmand. He is a glutton.' Rather, the banquet was to be seen and experienced as part of the theatre of international relations – Napoleon's chef creating a gastronomic spectacle for the conquering British monarch and his Russian allies.

Carême was perfecting at the Brighton Pavilion the philosophy of fine food presentation that he had begun to develop while working for Talleyrand. His genius was to deploy methods that brought out the natural flavours of food ('small vegetables should be cooked a little firm') – to create a gourmand's paradise – while at the same time producing a feast which could, visually, live up to the most opulent settings. By importing the decorative styles of the confectionery room to the main kitchen, the savoury courses regained a leading role in these meals. Carême thus looked backwards to the tradition of court chefs who best expressed themselves through grand *service à la français* presentation, and also forwards as the man who could lend respectability and élan to restaurant-style *service à la russe* by placing exquisitely presented and 'natural' tasting savoury food at the centre of the drama of eating. In *Maître d'hôtel*, which he published in 1822, he wrote:

I had remarked at the grand dinners of Prince Talleyrand that the larger pieces of cooked food for the first course never met the elegance of the bronzes, the glass, and the plate which covered the table at this period, so well as the elegant pastries of the time, the *entremets* of sugar, the cold entrées, and pastry-craft pedestals. Delivering myself entirely up to cookery, I promised myself that I would reform an infinity of old uses, though practised as they were by the greatest masters of the art. When I became *chef de cuisine* to Tsar Alexander, I commenced this great reform. But the mode of serving a Russian dinner was unfitted for it, all the *grosses pièces* being carved before being placed on the table... with the Prince Regent I was gratified, for this truly royal table was served always in the French manner, and the service of silver was so superb and elegant that I was struck with wonder; it appeared then that it would advance my reputation to commence the reform that I had proposed... thus it was to the Prince Regent of Great Britain that I presented for the first time 'Pike à la Régence' surrounded with rich garniture composed of fish of every description. My royal master and his noble guests remarked it, and complimented me: this encouragement flattered me, for I saw that I was right, and in this circumstance as in many others, my own thoughts were fruitful to me in the perfecting of culinary art...

Carême – and his food – so charmed the Prince Regent that on one occasion the prince visited the kitchens and arranged to eat there so that he could have a better feel of life 'below stairs'.

It should be noted that a red carpet was laid throughout the kitchens before his visit. The occasion was parodied by George Cruikshank in a cartoon which shows Carême guffawing in the background. Cruikshank's caption reads: 'a new Farce … lately performed at the Theatre Royal Brighton for the education and amusement of the cooks, scullions, dishwashers, trenchers, shoe-blacks, cinder-shifters, candle snuffers etc. etc. of that theatre, but which was unfortunately damned the first night by Common Sense!'

Carême's expression of bemused or amused horror in the cartoon may not be so far from the truth. His time in the service of the 'First Gentleman of Europe' – the 'Prince of Pleasures' – should have been the apotheosis of his career. But it was not. Despite the fact that his employer adored Carême's food and was able to supply him with the best produce, unsurpassed kitchens and a princely budget, and for all that Carême adored the lavish architecture which surrounded him, he was profoundly unhappy. He was hopelessly homesick, he later wrote, felt 'morally isolated' by the rest of the royal household, and had to beg to return to France less than 12 months after his arrival. Things had gone very wrong.

In fact, the year from 1816 through to 1817 had turned out to be an *annus horribilis* for the Royal Household, both above and below stairs, and for Carême in particular. The weather was so poor in 1816 that fires were lit in August, there was snow by early November, and the smog by early 1817 was so thick that John Philip Kemble, the celebrated actor, was forced to take opium to cope with his asthma on stage. Carême said he loathed these fogs – especially in Brighton – which exacerbated his growing respiratory problems.

The Regent led a peripatetic life and in the nine months, maybe more, that Carême worked for him he became very familiar with the old Dorking Road back and forth from Carlton House to the pleasure palace on Brighthelmstone Steine. It was a depressing journey as the roads were thick with mud from the incessant bad weather. And his spirits were rarely lifted when he arrived in Brighton, where the Pavilion remained, almost for the duration of his employment in the Royal household, a rain-soaked building site.

The working atmosphere in the Regent's kitchens proved no sunnier. The royal household was strictly delineated on class lines, and Antonin did not fit in well. His first surprise was to find that all the staff and retinue were expected to sign a household contract, known as the 'Book of Entitlement', granting them arcane perquisites such as candles or Yuletide mince-pies that had developed over time into real, financial privileges – for instance, the right to sell off unwanted food.

The kitchen entitlements from that period are still held in the royal archives. Carême's sous-chef Frederick Badua, for instance, had, 'in the year ending 6 January 1817', the rights to £16 16 shillings and 6 pence from the 'sale' of 20 loins of veal at 15 shillings each and 20 pounds of butter at 1 shilling and 10 pence, which is to say a near ten per cent annual bonus. The other top-paid chefs (though they earned only a tenth of

Antonin's salary) received an additional £19 or equivalent in alcohol, making a total bonus of £35 – as much as the whole year's pay of a Windsor page.

Although there had been some attempt to make reforms under George III, the Regent's father, to prevent deliberate over-catering, the entitlement system had for a long time worked fairly well. With meals served *à la française*, there was always a lot left over, and everyone could benefit according to their position. But then Carême arrived.

Rather than joining the system, he chose to maintain his 'freelance' status and did not sign the Book. He thus set himself apart from all the kitchen hierarchy. He, along with the other top chefs, sold off superfluous dishes, but he could do so unfettered by any concept of pooled profit: the money went straight into his own pocket.

And so it was that, in the winter of 1816–17, the kitchen staff found themselves accosted at the door by tradesmen offering to pay 'immense prices' for 'second-hand pâtés' as long as they had been made by the celebrated Carême himself. Carême outsold his colleagues, and undermined trade in the wares of those others who had greater need of the extra income, whilst working part-time hours and pocketing a £2,000 salary under the (dining) table. No wonder they hated him.

And it wasn't as if they weren't already under considerable strain, as they struggled to meet the Regent's – and Carême's – ever-increasing demands. Extra staff had to be hired. John

Lighthouse, the table-decker who worked in the decking room between the kitchen and dining-room at Brighton, gained an assistant, George Tweedy, who first appeared in the household archives in the quarter ending 5 April 1817. Two more kitchen boys, Charles Spring and John Miller, arrived, as well as more 'turnbroaches, door keepers and soil carriers' to clean out the 'two offices for butter and eggs, and greens'. In December 1816 new warrants for china and glass were issued to Hutchins, the royal tableware supplier, and in March 1817 a new roasting chef, Edward Jones, joined the staff.

Closer inspection of the records also reveals evidence of some sort of drama having unfolded around the bubbling stockpots. In spring 1817, the married under-cooks Michael and Sarah Ullersberger, who had been in service with the Prince for a decade, were dismissed summarily with all perquisites and rights withdrawn. What happened behind the Chinese doors to the Pavilion kitchens? Had the Ullersbergers fallen short of Antonin's famed perfectionism? Had his militaristic disinclination to employ women in his 'heroic' domain of the kitchen ruffled feathers? Or did something perhaps happen between Sarah Ullersberger and the increasingly lonely head chef?

Next page: 'High life Below Stairs', by Cruikshank. Reports that the Prince had dined with the servants in the Brighton kitchens made it into the Brighton Herald *after Carême's departure. Nevertheless, the laughing chef, far left, is traditionally said to represent Antonin*

London pub? by S W Fores 50 Piccadilly March 25 1810

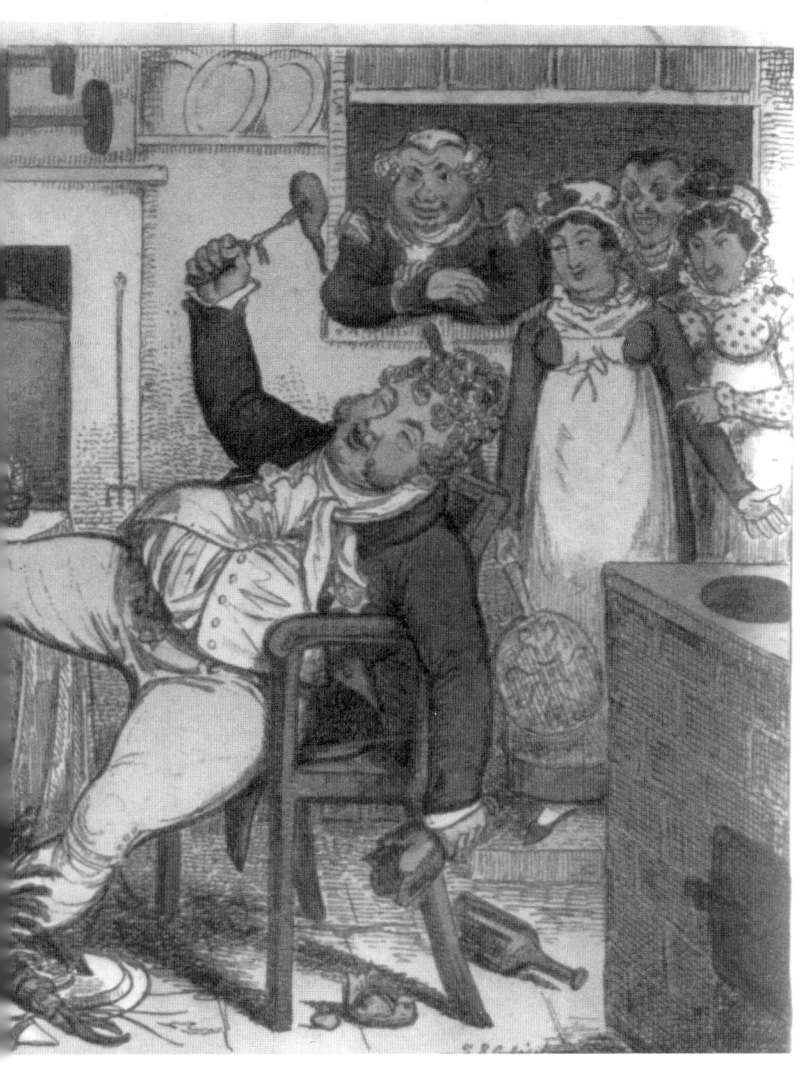

Carême doesn't tell us exactly, though pointedly he later claimed that by the end of his time in England none of the kitchen staff would talk to him, that he felt ostracised, 'morally isolated' and wretched.

He did explain that the lack of clear leadership in the kitchens was one problem. As was the alternation of responsibility between the top five chefs at Brighton and Carlton House and himself, and their inability, seemingly, to co-ordinate their time and space management. He criticised the English cooks for their over-reliance on Cayenne pepper and over-boiling of meat, and complained that there were too many women in the kitchen, for all he complimented their cooking. But he never explained precisely why things turned so bitter.

On one subject he was unequivocal, however: he hated the footmen – French or not – and said that, if things turned sour in the kitchen, he could never expect any below stairs friendship or complicity in the footmen's hall. 'Hypocritical valets,' he called them in the French style, 'are the death of a peaceful household; they are vain, arrogant, grovelling, lazy and unfit. They are worse than muskrats. Their lies capture the confidence of the masters, in order to make use of them when they need to. The valet who believes himself an equal is a fool. They are the Tartuffes of Domesticity.' Like many chefs, he had a distrust bordering on the paranoid about his waiting staff. 'Would you please tread softly,' he would hiss at the footmen as they carried his desserts through the blue-tiled servants' corridor at Brighton to the decking and dining-rooms, 'Carry carefully *and lift your feet!*'

Life 'above stairs' was no less stormy. Carême later confessed that he had felt uncomfortable at Brighton as close witness to the '*bourgeois ménage*' that existed as the Prince Regent vacillated between the ample charms of Lady Hertford and Lady Conyngham. To make matters worse, his time in England coincided almost exactly with the marriage, pregnancy and death of the Prince Regent's heir, the Princess of Wales.

Young Charlotte, Princess of Wales – 'England's ONLY Hope' – was at one time intended for Archduke Nicholas of Russia, who ate so well at Brighton and Carlton House thanks to Carême. In the end she fell headlong for a member of Tsar Alexander's retinue when he visited England after leaving Antonin in Paris in 1814. This was Prince Leopold of Saxe-Coburg (uncle of both Prince Albert and Queen Victoria). When the betrothed couple came to stay at Brighton for Christmas of 1816, the onion domes of the Pavilion had to be turned into makeshift dormitories for the ranks of extra servants.

Antonin cooked the festive meals, and the princess who had at last found happiness after a childhood scarred by her parents' bitter marriage lost her habitual stammer, to general rejoicing. By the following November she was dead, victim to the scourge of Regency women: poor obstetrics. The court and country went into shocked mourning, flooding the palace with offers of money for a memorial – embezzled by her 'distraught' father, who sought solace, it was said, only in food – and Sir Richard Croft, the unfortunate accoucheur, shot himself. Antonin returned to France.

—«◆»—

CARÊME REMAINED FOREVER intrigued by this first experience of foreign travel, and took trouble to note down what had struck him as unusual. Only because of him do we know, for instance, that in 1816 truffles did not grow naturally in the United Kingdom; that beef was of a much higher quality in London than Paris; that chicken was adulterated by unscrupulous butchers with chalk to whiten the meat, turning it black on cooking; that mushrooms were preserved in lemon juice; and that the fowl on English dining-tables maintained a superior textural quality to their Continental cousins because they were suffocated at Smithfield Market rather than strangled, hung or garrotted.

It had been an unhappy year, though, for the Regency court, and an unhappy year for Carême. 'Each day,' he said, 'the differences between our two countries – so similar and yet so foreign to each other – become clearer and I [feel] increasingly not so much a homesickness as sickness of soul.'

He wrote, perhaps ironically, that he knew he would never find a situation as 'sweet or as beautiful' as in the Regent's household but that his 'soul belonged to France', to which he returned in late 1817 with no clear plans of what to do next.

POTAGE DE KARIE À L'INDIENNE

This Curry Soup was served to Archduke Nicholas of
Russia at the Brighton Pavilion on 18 January 1817.
Carême created several such soups, inspired by the
architecture of the Pavilion.

In a deep dish cover two small chickens with
sufficient chicken stock (about three pints) and.
surround with slices of fatty bacon and also: a
bunch of parsley, two bay leaves, four cloves, a
pinch of mace, a pinch of Cayenne pepper, a pinch
of allspice, pepper, thyme and basil. Boil for three-
quarters of an hour. Remove the chickens and strain
the consommé into a pan containing ten ounces of
rice. Add a slight infusion of saffron to achieve a
delicate yellow. Boil for an hour. Cut the chicken
into small pieces and pour the hot soup over the
chicken in a tureen before serving. Despite the taste
of the English, Cayenne should not dominate the
flavour of the soup.

Antonin Carême

CHAPTER 10

Viennoiserie

Only the wisest men know the art of good eating

Brillat-Savarin

arême, now aged 34, was too much in demand to be idle for long. Shortly after his return to the French capital, he was sought out by the comptroller of the imperial Russian household, Muller, who was passing through Paris with Tsar Alexander on their way to Aix-la-Chapelle for the 1818 Peace Congress. A new European Alliance was to be created, in the hope that this would avoid another war. It was to give post-Napoleonic Europe 'the efficiency and almost the simplicity of a single state', wrote the British Foreign Minister Lord Castlereagh. The language of diplomacy had been French since the Middle Ages, but after the 1814–15 Congress of Vienna there was an expectation that diplomats would be fed in the new French manner, too. Muller convinced the Tsar that Carême's cooking would help the Russian cause.

Antonin agreed to travel to Aix for 2,400 francs a month (a reduction on his Brighton wage), but with a lavish monthly budget of 100,000 francs. Since it was unclear how long the conference would last, Muller suggested that Carême should be appointed as the Tsar's chef with the idea that he would travel on to St Petersburg afterwards. Antonin, fresh from his unsatisfactory experiences in the Prince Regent's household, agreed to go to Aix but would not commit himself further.

After the decadent chaos of Brighton's '*ménage bourgeois*', Carême was relieved to find that the imperial household was organised with almost military precision – no sudden changes of mealtimes while the Prince Regent adjusted his necktie. 'My manner pleased the Emperor,' boasted Antonin, 'which was not difficult as everything in the great house of the Tsar was dignified and truly imperial.'

Muller hoped that the lavish munificence of the Romanovs' dining habits would tempt Carême to travel with them back to Russia. In Aix, for example, Carême's budget allowed him to serve Sicilian oranges, Ostende oysters, Volga sturgeon, Périgord truffles, English strawberries and both pineapples and hothouse cherries at one meal – and all in December. But Carême was resistant to all blandishments.

While in Aix, he met again the diplomats he had served when he was working for Talleyrand – Nesselrode, Metternich and Castlereagh – and, more fortuitously, he cooked again for Castlereagh's food-loving brother, Lord Charles Stewart.

Unexpectedly, it was Stewart who won the prize as the next employer of Antonin Carême.

Charles Stewart (1778–1854) had just been appointed British ambassador to Vienna. The dandy who had made something of an ass of himself at the Congress of 1814–15, fighting with cab drivers and goosing debutantes at the opera, was maturing into a respectable diplomat. He was also about to marry one of the richest young heiresses in London, Lady Frances Anne Vane-Tempest.

Like Carême's previous employers, Talleyrand and the Prince Regent, Stewart loved a uniform. He wore them well. One of his several conquests in Vienna in 1814, the Duchesse de Sagan, had nicknamed him the 'Golden Pheasant' for his love of yellow riding boots and 'Big Lord Pumpernickel' for reasons unrecorded. 'His nature was chivalrous,' eulogised one of Stewart's admirers, though the Austrian secret police thought otherwise. They called him a '*sabreur*': a swordsman, a blade… or indeed a bungler (which was exactly how Byron described the Castlereaghs in the preface to *Don Juan*). Still, Stewart had the Castlereagh good looks, a rakish scar from a close encounter with musket-shot at the Battle of Donauwörth – and a good deal more humour than his brother.

Lady Frances Anne Vane-Tempest, who was 19 when she met Lord Charles, was heiress to a fortune based on coalmines in Teesside and a hereditary Anglo-Irish earldom. She and Lord Charles were introduced at a dinner party in Bruton Street, Mayfair, in 1818. They married soon afterwards.

Antonin dedicated several of his books to the Stewarts, writing about them in terms that are gushing, even given the sycophantic style of the period. Milord was 'handsome, polite, spiritual, intelligent, loyal, generous… and a great lover of the table'. Antonin also approved of his wife – as well he might. It was her fortune that enabled Stewart to afford the world's most expensive chef.

The Stewarts set themselves up in regal style in Vienna, giving Antonin a large budget and a large staff under his direct control. 'For a young lord,' said Antonin, 'an Embassy is a course in gastronomy as much as in diplomacy.' Antonin recorded every detail of the menus he served in the ambassadorial residence on Minoritenplatz, complaining about the poor standards in Austrian abattoirs but exulting in the quality of Bavarian pheasant. Served under leather cloches and directly on to the plate, these menus are arrestingly modern – already much more recognisable as the *haute cuisine* of a modern restaurant than Antonin's gargantuan feasts in Paris.

DINNER SERVED TO LORD AND LADY STEWART
AT MINORITENPLATZ, VIENNA

POTAGE

Turtle Madeira soup

༄

RELEVÉ DE POISSON

Salmon in champagne

༄

ONE GROSSE PIÈCE

Roast beef garnished with horseradish

༄

TWO ENTRÉES

Lamb chops, puréed potatoes
Capons with a béchamel sauce

༄

A PLATE OF ROASTS

Goslings with puréed apples

༄

FOUR ENTREMETS

Grilled mushrooms
Stuffed cucumbers
Orange fromage bavarois
Strawberry tartelettes

The Stewarts, with Carême in their kitchens, were popular hosts in Vienna, though considered slightly eccentric, with their Turkish pages dressed in tunics and turbans. They both loved the theatre and after dinner would insist on their guests taking part in amateur dramatics, despite 'no one having any idea of acting'. But their first posting in Vienna was short-lived. Crown business soon forced Stewart to return to England. Throughout his diplomatic career in Europe, Stewart had been obliged to solicit incriminating evidence on a fellow Continental roustabout, Caroline, the Princess of Wales, the estranged wife of the Prince Regent; and the fruits of this 'research' were now being turned to account. The Prince was suing for divorce.

Antonin followed the Stewarts to London. But few details have survived of his second sojourn in England – except for a recipe for partridge soup, which he records as having devised at Lady Frances's family home of Wynyard Park in County Durham (a place he seems unlikely to have visited except in his imagination, as he describes it as being on 'the frontier with Ireland').

By the early summer of 1819, however, he was back in Paris. He had been sent an offer he could no longer refuse.

PARTRIDGE SOUP À LA STEWART

'This savoury soup is very much to the
taste of English lords'

Wash a quart of lentils and put them in a soup pot with a slice of ham, a fowl and two partridges. Moisten the whole with some good consommé, add two carrots, two onions and a head of celery, a bunch of chervil, seasoned with a fragment of bay leaf, thyme, marjoram, a little pepper, grated nutmeg and two cloves. When it boils, skim and place on a low fire for four hours. Take all the fat off and take up the fowl and the partridges. Take off all their flesh and pound thoroughly to rub them through a sieve with the lentils. Remove the ham and chervil. Then place the purée in a soup pot in a bain-marie, that it may not boil, and when serving pour it into the tureen upon some quenelles of partridges.

Antonin Carême

CHAPTER 11

The Winter Palace

Whatever partings destiny may bring,
Whatever fortunes fate may have in hand,
We are still the same: the world to us a foreign thing,
And Tsarskoe Selo our only Fatherland.

Alexander Pushkin, *Polnoe sobranie sochinenii*

A letter followed Carême in that spring of 1819 from Paris to Vienna to Paris and eventually reached him at the Stewart residence in St James's Square, London. It was from Prince Orlov in St Petersburg. The letter offered Carême the choice of two posts in the Russian Imperial Household; as Maitre d' or Head Chef. Antonin felt in need of advice: he took the post chaise from London to Paris – overnight a guinea-and-a-half per person and sixpence tip to the crew – and in Paris met up with an old friend.

The French chef, Monsieur Daniel, had just returned from St Petersburg. He had made a great deal of money there, and encouraged Antonin to do the same. It is unclear whether Tsar Alexander's famous remark, '*he deserves his fortune for he has taught us to eat*', was in fact made about Carême, the chef Riquette or the chef Daniel, all of whom made big money in Russia and bigger impressions on Russian cooking. In any event, Antonin, the reluctant traveller, this time seems not to have hesitated to leave France. If he saw Agathe and his little daughter Marie while he was in Paris, he makes no mention of it. He set out for Honfleur and the sail-packet to Russia.

Antonin abhorred sea travel. It was dangerous of course in the early 1800s – dirty, unreliable and frightening. But his distaste seems to have been as old as the sea itself; he got seasick. His passage to Russia was a particularly cruel one. At first, as the densely packed masts of Honfleur harbour disappeared from view, Antonin was relieved to find a complete calm holding the sea. But this lasted all the way to the Baltic, and greatly slowed their wind-powered progress. There were insufficient provisions on board and the king of chefs was obliged to eat with the sailors – salt-cod and biscuits. Near Elsinore, on the Danish coast, a storm hit the ship, and by the time they entered the relative calm of the Gulf of Finland, Antonin declared that he was 'dying'.

The journey was not yet over. The storm continued and Antonin, like many visitors to St Petersburg in rough weather, landed first at Kronstadt Island – then as now a grim outpost guarding the approach to the 'Venice of the North' – where he remained marooned for over a week. It would have been a particularly frustrating wait. There was little to do in the military fortress, and little to eat apart from the local vobla fish that the naval cadets hung to dry in their windows. Moreover, the view of the St Petersburg stage-set from across the water was tantalisingly close. Peter the Great's new capital for Russia presented – still presents – its best and most awe-inspiring façade to the sea. The gilded spires and domes of the Peter-Paul Fortress, the Winter Palace and the naval and St Isaac's cathedrals draw the eye up from the grey waters of the Neva estuary like the perspective tricks of 18th-century opera.

Eventually, the seas calmed and Antonin braved the last waves across the Neva to the monumental Romanov Winter Palace. St Petersburg in 1819 was a modern city. For an aspiring architect like Carême it was the ideal modern capital, mapped out on a grid of canals and streets with the resources of an autocratic empire to requisition lavish building materials, and demand cohesive design. The palaces along the Fontanka Canal are laid out, in the same symmetrical principle as *service à la française*, according to prescribed ideas of the effect of the whole. They are also prescribed according to the rank of their then owners, and this St Petersburg style, of grandeur and control, both impressed and slightly alarmed Carême as it had so many before and since.

The Winter Palace, St Petersburg. Of all the palaces in Europe, only Versailles was bigger. As Carême was greeted by Riquette at the Neva steps to the palace, the Tsar, unaware of his arrival, was leaving on the other side of the building

He may at first have been comforted by the ubiquity of his compatriots. The City of Palaces was full of the French: French architects and artists, governesses and courtesans, tutors and cooks welcomed the famous chef when he finally arrived. But he soon found that among the Russian nobility for whom he would cook, there had been a sea change in opinion since 1812 and Napoleon's invasion. Among the younger generation, in particular, like Prince Orlov and Prince Volkonsky, it was newly fashionable to be suspicious of French imports.

Prince Sergei Volkonsky was Carême's first point of contact when he arrived in St Petersburg. No longer just aide-de-camp as in France but on home soil the de facto head of the Imperial Household, he represented perfectly the dual response that Carême met to French influences in Russian culture and cooking. Volkonsky was a Francophile by nurture, like any Russian aristocrat, but the disastrous Napoleonic invasion had scarred his attitude to France, and to Russia's over-reliance on Western influences.

The Russians were busily rediscovering their non-European heritage. This extended from dancing the *pliaska* rather than the waltz, and drinking vodka rather than claret, to preferring borsch to Carême's style of imported French cuisine. For this reason, Russian cooking ultimately influenced Carême more than he it – though he was able to have some impact on its development (he is credited, for instance, with introducing cream as an alternative to vinegar in Russian sauces – a partial victory it must be said). Meanwhile, Volkonsky had specific bad news for Carême. The Tsar had had to go to Arkangel and requested that Antonin wait indefinitely for his return.

Antonin felt stranded and let down. For the moment, he decided, he would stay; he could not then have foreseen how alien, and challenging, he would find the below stairs world of Russia in 1819. The staffing in St Petersburg was unparalleled even in Carême's wide experience. In an age when the live-in staff of the Duke of Devonshire at Chatsworth could number as little as 18, and there were rarely more than three times that number 'backstage' at the Brighton Pavilion, any of the dozens of aristocratic establishments in Petersburg could expect to house several hundred below stairs staff. Antonin discovered that a mere steward in the Tsar's household could have responsibility for over a thousand underlings. These were not all fellow servants. They were serfs. Their status is confirmed by a contemporary St Petersburg advertisement for a kitchen maid 'to be sold, aged 16 years, of good behaviour, and a second-hand carriage, slightly used'. With these hundreds of workers in the kitchens and elsewhere, the potential for corruption was enormous, and indeed when Carême arrived he found that because of recent abuses of privileges in the numerous palace kitchens – misappropriation of funds, food and gifts – all the kitchen staff were under suspicion. An audit was in progress.

The military precision that Carême had observed in the Tsar's households at the Elysée and Aix veered, during the 1819 Winter Palace audit, towards the martinet. It was, he complained, humiliating. Everything he used had to be accounted for, as if he were a serf. Worse still, he was under constant surveillance.

Carême's reaction of distress at the Winter Palace seems disproportionate to the simple professional inconvenience of being audited. The extent to which he was under surveillance, he claimed, offended his sense of honour. But in fact there was probably more to it than that. The Russians had other reasons for watching the chef. They thought he might be a spy. This rumour dogged Antonin throughout his international career, and especially in Russia, and as an acolyte of Talleyrand it is not difficult to see why. However there is no evidence in the scant records in St Petersburg, Moscow or Paris that any suspicion was justified. Despite his celebrity status and his occasional conversations with politicians and royalty, he was no better placed than any other expatriate Frenchman to indulge in a bit of espionage. So he could probably feel justifiably indignant at being watched and held to account.

But there were some distinct upsides to Antonin's experience in Russia. He was not as lonely there as he had been in Brighton: the Paris chefs Riquette and Benois were in St Petersburg as well as Talon, Dubois and the younger Masse, all of them profiting by a new 'fusion' of Russian and French cuisine. And he used his time productively. He did much more than his French friends claimed, who scoffed that he simply checked if the gates of the Summer Gardens were really topped with gold (they are) and left – like the

Englishman in the Russian fable. His later work, *Projects for the Architectural Embellishment of St Petersburg*, makes it clear that he toured the city with a sketch pad and made notes on the public spaces that, to his confectioner's eye, could do with some 'embellishment'. He also studied the produce available. Pacing the granite embankments, he discovered a fascinating novelty for sale on the streets: frozen food. He was impressed by the range and quality of fruit available, though surprised by how expensive it was. He was appalled to discover that cherries could cost several roubles a pound, and astounded at Petersburg extravagance, witnessing a meal hosted by 'an opulent young man' at which a whole cherry tree in fruit was placed in the centre of the table – costing 1,800 roubles. He also noted how the French chefs in St Petersburg were entirely reliant for half the year on hothouse vegetables. These did not have the taste of their seasonally grown counterparts; 'My eyes tell me I am eating asparagus but my mouth is not convinced,' wrote one contemporary of Russian-ripened produce. Even so Antonin was overwhelmed by the magnificence of the greenhouses of the Tauride Palace – where the Muscat vines planted by Catherine the Great and her lover Potemkin still flourished – and naturally enough by the quality and quantity of fish and caviar.

Foreigners always stand outside the local class-structure, and Carême's status in St Petersburg was as an international celebrity rather than an imperial servant. The truth was that he found himself more socially mobile in autocratic

Russia than he had ever been in post-Revolutionary France: he was even, on one occasion, invited to dinner as a guest of a Prince.

The evening did not get off to the best start. The footman who announced him mispronounced Carême's name, and the Russian aristocrats – who would all have been more fluent in French than their 'native' Russian – made a point of laughing. He was then placed next to a garrulous Russian general – though in the end this probably suited him very well. While the general perorated, Antonin could do what he loved most – observe and note every detail of the decorations and music. The table was dressed with flowers and fruit, in the Russian manner, but there was no knowing from the menu cards, as there would have been in France, what one was actually going to eat. The *grosses pièces* – a beef, an Arkangel veal (the best according to Carême), a Volga sturgeon and a turkey – were first displayed to the guests and then taken away and re-presented, on the plate, hot. Antonin noted this approvingly; a sort of hybrid of *service à la française* and *service à la russe* styles. However, the constant changing of plates exposed everyone, he felt, to the danger of uncleanliness. He could not believe there was enough crockery to replace 20 plates for all 40 guests, and assumed therefore that the plates were being hastily washed and returned. In fact the staffing – and porcelain – of a Russian palace could well allow such laborious extravagance. Antonin also noted the age-old Russian habit of making toasts between courses and admired the rum sorbets served to 'renew the appetite'. On the whole he approved of his one recorded experience on the other side of the green baize doors. The only thing he objected to seriously was the music – 60 serf musicians in a neighbouring room who played 'from soup until the last dessert wine', forcing everyone to shout.

Peterhof Palace, half a day by sailboat from St Petersburg, boasts that Carême cooked there. Perhaps he did, and it certainly has a proud place in the history of conspicuous Russian consumption. At the supper given there to celebrate the birth of Alexander I by his grandmother Catherine the Great, there was a dessert garnished 'with jewels to the amount of upwards two million pounds sterling'. Her lover Prince Potemkin entertained lavishly there as elsewhere. He once spent 20,000 roubles – enough it was said to build a small palace – on a dinner and entertainment which included a soup of rare sterlet (a type of sturgeon) costing 3,000 roubles and served in a silver bathtub. The Hermitage in the gardens at Peterhof had a pulley-system *deus ex machina* that could raise an entire dining-table, set with food, from the kitchens into the dining-room – a huge advance on Antonin's Valençay dumb-waiter. Carême, however, is said to have cooked in the kitchens of the Catherine Wing at the Palace. This 'wing' or pavilion comprises a set of rooms which were decorated for Alexander in Carême's time. They include a serving-room with plate-warmer in the style of a Russian house-stove that is said to be unique in Russia and certainly suggests some serious attention to food in 1819. There is also a narrow kitchen, radically restored after the Nazi bombardment, and a 6,000-piece Gureyev porcelain service which dates precisely from Antonin's arrival. In post-1812 style, the plates were decorated with Russian, not classical or French scenes, but the service also included hundreds of high-standing pedestals for the *grosses pièces* and *pièces montées* that Carême had made famous.

With the Tsar in Arkangel, and St Petersburg society newly ambivalent to imported French styles, Carême was potentially underemployed. However, one Romanov remained redolently Francophile and did invite him to cook: the Dowager Empress. Maria Feodorovna (1759–1828), like her son Alexander, was erudite, spirited – and, according to the American President John Quincy Adams, among others – still handsome in old age. After the murder of her husband, Maria Feodorovna spent much of her time at the elegant summer palace, part of the complex of palaces at Tsarskoe Selo outside Petersburg, which was named Pavlovsk after her husband.

Pavlovsk had become a rival court to that of the absentee Tsar when he was in Paris or on campaign. In marked contrast to the Brobdingnagian glitter of the other Tsarskoe Selo palaces, it was a temple of French-style neoclassicism. he admired. Elements of its interior décor were familiar to him

Dowager Empress Maria Feodorovna (1759–1828), widow of Tsar Paul I. Even Marie Antoinette described her as 'stiff'

from Brighton, a hybrid of *exotique* styles including Egyptian, Here Maria Feodorovna held 'salons' for French-speaking artists such as le Brun, Gonzaga and Carlo Rossi, and the historian Karamzin. They called Pavlovsk 'Parnassus', but it was also known as a temple of fine – French – food. It was the only one of the Romanov palaces that Carême acknowledged and the overall impression was one of elegance and even femininity. Its kitchens, however, did not meet with his approval. They had been designed so that one had to negotiate a steep, curved flight of stairs with the food.

Carême arrived for the name-day of the Empress in 1819, a court and family occasion with over a hundred guests. For meals like this, the lapis lazuli Sèvres service was used, a gift from Marie Antoinette in happier times when, together, she and Maria Feodorovna – on an *incognito* visit to France under the pseudonym 'Countess of the North' – had visited the Sèvres factory. The French queen is by tradition credited with the shape of Sèvres porcelain cups: they are said to be modelled on her breasts.

Maria Feodorovna's birthday-party guests sat in the white dining-room, overlooking the temples and follies of the garden, and arranged, Antonin said, around a horseshoe-shaped dining-table. Above them, in a detail said to mock Maria Feodorovna's imperious mother-in-law, Catherine the Great, white plaster Medusas stared down. The table was groaning with flowers, and there was a further Russian tradition that earned Antonin's ringing endorsement: 'At the Romanov court the head chef – there are four on fortnightly shifts – always serve dinner themselves, as *maître d'hôtel*. This should be adopted by gourmet-kings everywhere.'

At Carême's dinner the Dowager Empress was dressed in an ostrich-plumed toque and long gloves. Her mealtime ritual that evening was as unbending as her famously over-corseted torso. One footman first removed her chair and replaced it under her. A second presented a gold tray for her gloves and fan. Without looking back, she reached for the jewelled pin which she knew would be waiting in the hands of the third footman, and with this she pinned her napkin next to the Maltese cross of her late husband at her neck. Even Marie Antoinette had described her as 'stiff'.

That evening, dinner was served *à la russe*, though Carême later said that this did not suit the dishes prepared. In his opinion a grand presentation *à la française* would have been preferable. More than French chauvinism was at stake. At Pavlovsk, the octagonal serving-room from which the birthday banquet was served opened draftily at every corner on to all the principal rooms of the palace. Serving *à la russe* from this room would have caused almost every dish, already cooling after a journey up from the kitchens, to drop further in temperature.

On grand occasions at Pavlovsk, guests were greeted on the road by the students of Tsar Alexander's *lycée*, all in their Sunday best of blue, red and gold. On Maria Feodorovna's name-day in 1819, as Antonin watched the guests arriving, an

18-year-old schoolboy tossed his hat in the air and cheered. The town once called Tsarskoe Selo now bears the boy's name: Alexander Pushkin.

After that party Antonin never saw the Empress again. He tired of the strange Romanov court, and of waiting for the Tsar through the perpetual daylight of St Petersburg's 1819 white-nights. 'I saw things as they were,' he said, 'and decided to put honour before interest, and quit Russia.' He re-embarked for Kronstadt and for France.

The troubled Tsar, meanwhile, was to retreat more and more into the mysticism that had turned Carême's Vertus banquet into a Eucharist. In 1825 he died unexpectedly. Some say it was food poisoning, some typhus, some syphilis from wilder times above Carême's kitchens at Hôtel Talleyrand and the Elysée. Most Russians believe that Alexander faked his own death to spend the rest of his days eating rye bread, an ascetic hermit in the Urals. It is said that when the Bolsheviks opened the coffin a hundred years later, they found it empty.

The effect of Carême on Russia and Russia on Carême is a subject that belies the relatively short time he spent there. In Russia, Carême is famous for the introduction of cream sauces, and supposedly for successfully ridding Russian cooks of their over-reliance on pickling. The proud tradition of Franco-Russian cooking before the Russian Revolution owed a great deal to the French chefs of St Petersburg and Moscow, and even more to their reliance on Carême's books.

Conversely, Carême's time with the Romanov court came to influence Western cooking. It was he who encouraged the Russian-style use of flowers where porcelain and fruit had dominated table decoration, and he who imported to France borsch and koulibiac (a pie with either fish or chicken, boiled eggs and rice – variously called *coulibiac* or *koulibiaca*. The authentic Eastern European version is topped with the spinal marrow of sturgeon). And his endorsement of *service à la russe* – though not dominant till later in the 19th century – affects the way we eat to this day. But more vitally, in terms of his publishing and cooking careers, Carême returned to France with a reputation gilded by association with the most modern and glamorous of capitals and kings.

The return journey was yet more hellish than the outbound. Carême's ship, unable to dock, was buffeted for 38 days between Calais and Boulogne in full view of other recent wrecks. The captain was injured, and then his second-in-command, and by the time they could put in at Calais they had neither mast nor sails. In salt-cured clothes Antonin went to the portside church to give thanks, and spent several days recovering before continuing to Paris.

RUSSIAN SOUP

As served by Carême,
from a traditional Russian recipe

Cut in small pieces three pounds of brisket of beef, and one pound of streaky bacon. Put these in a stockpot covered with beef stock and boil for two hours. Then add two onions sliced, and sweated in butter, a spoonful of flour, and a white cabbage cut up, washed, and drained. Boil these two hours. Add six sausages, which take up again ten minutes afterwards, skim the soup and serve. This is the common soup of the Russian people.

Antonin Carême

CHAPTER 12

'Right good judges and right good stuffers'

For a great diplomat to maintain his position he must employ a great cook.

Antonin Carême

In the complicated sexual roundelay of Carême's employers, two women were central. The Duchesse de Sagan and the Princess Bagration had both in their time slept with Talleyrand, Stewart, Metternich and the Tsar, who, in his turn, was in love with Frances Stewart. Princess Katerina Pavlovna Skavronska Bagration, was notorious as the *'bel ange nu'*, a reference to her scandalously scanty ball-gowns. But by the time Carême came to work for her in Paris in late 1819, fashions had changed and so had her figure – for after rich men, the princess's other earthy delight was rich food.

'La Grande Bagration', as she became known, was Latvian in origin. She had been married to a Russian war hero, had

had a child by Metternich and a tumultuous affair with Tsar Alexander, so that, when she appeared once as the Virgin Mary in a *tableau vivant* after a Carême dinner, there was much comment on her skill – as an actress. In any other age she might have been a politician. In Antonin's day, she hosted dinners and salons for the Parisian political and literary set and made her influence felt indirectly.

'At table she had a grace, a charm in conversation that should serve as a model,' wrote Antonin, who was able to observe this personally now that he insisted on the Russian manner of serving at table, his sword by his side. 'I served always as *maître d'hôtel* [for the princess] and I was always complimented.'

The princess's flirtatious ways were not lost on Antonin. 'Carême,' she teased, 'you say I am capricious in my tastes but it is not so. You see I am enchanted by your changing menus and I unswervingly accept them as you offer them.'

One evening the Princess overheard one of her guests boasting at having been at a Carême dinner. 'There must be some mistake,' she said, 'for I am sure he no longer cooks except for me.'

'Well,' rejoined her guest, 'this chef was a pearl.'

'A pearl he may have been, but he was a false pearl and mine is real.'

Antonin ends his record of this conversation rather gauchely: *'Et j'étais là!'*

He wasn't there for very long, however. The fat princess's health was not good, for all she told Talleyrand it had improved as a result of Carême. She fell into a sort of 'almost total inactivity' (it is only surprising that more of Carême's employers did not do the same) and took to her bed.

At the same time a letter arrived from Lord Stewart, which had gone, in the way of much of Carême's post, via Russia. Stewart had heard that after his stay in St Petersburg Carême had declined both of the positions on offer at the Winter Palace. The letter enquired after his availability, and touchingly contained the plaintive line from Stewart: 'I remain unable to find a chef who can live up to your memory.' With the Princess now too ill to make use of any chef, Carême asked for her permission to rejoin Lord Stewart – a request she accepted with suitable grace.

There is some confusion over the exact date of when Antonin joined Ambassador Stewart in Laybach. He was due, he later wrote, to meet him there and then travel with him to Vienna in 1820. But he seemed fated, as with the Tsar, to arrive just when he was not needed – or so he claimed. For when he reached Laybach, he found that Lord Stewart had left the night before to return to Vienna.

According to Antonin this was because the one-time 'sabreur' was skipping government business to join his young wife who had gone into labour. But in fact the baby, Charles Vane-Tempest-Stewart, was born in Vienna in 1821, the year after Antonin arrived. Was Antonin simply misremembering dates? Or was he rather, in the dedicated tradition of the discreet manservant, attempting to cover his rakish master's tracks?

Antonin actually left very little record of his activities in 1820 and 1821. This was because he was again preparing a book – or rather books. *Projects for the Architectural Embellishment of St Petersburg* might sound like an unlikely sequel to a cookery bestseller. It was. Exquisitely drawn by Carême and a draftsman called Percier who had given him drawing lessons, it featured statuary and monuments that were, in a sense, ahead of their time. They fit the magpie grandiosity of the mid-Victorians, of the Albert Memorial. Elephants, pyramids, arches and sphinxes are mixed in with Corinthian, Ionic and Gothic styles, such that, had St Petersburg ever been 'embellished' in the manner Carême suggested, no square or embankment would have been left un-follied. Carême engaged the finest firm of printers for this project, Firmin Didot Père et Fils, and the best engravers in Paris, Normand and Hibron. Flush with the dream of a future in architecture, he wrote to the Tsar, requesting permission to dedicate the book to him.

Sadly, it did not sell well. Nor did its sister volume, *Projects for the Architectural Embellishment of Paris* (published in 1826). Throughout the 1830s and 1840s they were repeatedly advertised in the later editions of his cookbooks, but always at an exorbitant 50 francs when his recipe books never cost more than 16 francs and even these sold better when they were priced at 10.

Like a modern bestseller writer, Antonin was straitjacketed by the expectations based on the early success of

Le Pâtissier royal parisien. The public only wanted to read recipes – and royal anecdotes – from Carême. Fortunately, he was also preparing a major work on household catering, *Maître d'hôtel français* which came out in 1822. It would secure his fortune.

Meanwhile, Antonin continued cooking for Stewart in Vienna at the Ambassador's residence at Minoritenplatz. And it was here, in Stewart's kitchens, that the 'chef's hat' was born. Each morning at 11 o'clock, he and the Ambassador met to discuss the evening meal, according to the custom Antonin had established at both Valençay and the Brighton Pavilion. Unlike Talleyrand or the Prince Regent, however, Lord Stewart met his celebrity chef in the kitchens – Carême's domain. And here, in 1821, he first noticed a difference in his chef's appearance. Antonin had taken to wearing a raised hat, a sort of toque, in contrast to the white nightcaps usually worn in kitchens in those days. When Stewart, in his halting French, asked why, Antonin said he felt a chef should not dress as for a sickbed – perhaps after the unfortunate demise of *La Grande Bagration* who never recovered from the 'almost total inactivity' that overcame her on her diet of pure Carême.

Antonin's insistence on stiffening his white hat was imitated first by the chefs of Vienna, then Paris, and then everywhere. Antonin later published an illustration of the cap, stiffened with a round of cardboard and later still he even suggested – in an early example of celebrity-chef product endorsement

– the best place to buy one: the *bonnetier* M. Pannier, on the boulevard de la Madeleine in Paris.

At one morning kitchen conference, Stewart's arrival was met with especial excitement. The staff knew a missive had arrived by diplomatic courier bearing the double-headed eagle of the Romanov court. It was for Carême, in response to his request to dedicate his book on St Petersburg to the Tsar. The Tsar graciously accepted the dedication, wrote Prince Volkonsky, and enclosed a ring, studded round with diamonds, as a gift for Carême.

The boy from the Paris gutters made some play of insouciance at being the recipient of Romanov largesse, but later admitted his pleasure that the 'ring was the subject of universal curiosity amongst my colleagues'. A portrait of Antonin from this period, the only known likeness in oils, features his right hand draped nonchalantly but prominently into the foreground. It bears a huge ring on the index finger. A large red gem is studded round with diamonds – shown more clearly in the engraving of the portrait that graced his later publications. Antonin asked his publishers in Paris to send a copy of the dedicated *Projects for the Architectural Embellishment of St Petersburg* to Tsar Alexander, but it never reached the library of The Hermitage. The journey to Russia, as Carême knew all

Carême's own depiction of chefs before and after his intended make-over of the uniform. The chef on the right wears the new-style toque 'stiffened with cardboard'. It is taken to be a self-portrait

too well, was hazardous. The ship was wrecked, and Carême's bid for an architecture commission from the Romanov court lies at the bottom of the Baltic Sea.

The ring was not the only precious gift to come Antonin's way in Vienna. 'A little while after [the gift of the ring] I created five great trophies in mastic representing the arms of the five Allied Powers,' he wrote in *Maître d'hôtel français*. 'These trophies were placed on five great glass pedestals and were the centrepiece of one of the most magnificent suppers I have ever executed. All the highest nobility of the land and from abroad, and the diplomatic corps were guests. The next morning, at the levée of Milady… one of the loveliest and best ladies, Milord Stewart asked me to the salon where I received more praise… The couple offered me a superb gold snuff-box.'

Carême's '*tabatière*' was in recognition of the huge success both of the meal and of the mastic trophies. The Stewarts then sent him on the short journey to Metternich's palace on Ballhausplatz with the German-themed sugar-paste trophy, as a gift for the prince 'to admire it at his ease'. The gold snuff-box was referred to thereafter as the 'Metternich *tabatière*'.

For many in the Vienna household the most memorable of Carême's meals was the christening dinner for the little Charles Stewart. The 'heiress's heir' George Henry Robert Charles William Vane-Tempest-Stewart, later Earl Vane, Baron Castlereagh and Marquess of Londonderry, blamed a lifetime of dental decay on his early childhood in Vienna and his parents' celebrated chef – though, naturally enough, he had no memory of Carême's finer services in his honour, such as this Christening banquet.

CHRISTENING DINNER
SERVED IN VIENNA

22 June 1821

(48 covers in the dining-room,

70 covers in the Gallery,

and 48 in the Throne Room.

This is the menu from the dining-room, for 48)

TWO SOUPS

Curried turtle soup

Rice soup à la Celestine

TWO FISH RELEVÉS

Salmon, Genovese sauce

Sturgeon au bleu, Provençale sauce

FOUR GROSSES PIÈCES

Chicken à la Montmorency

Filets of bœuf à la Périgueux

Glazed ham on a pedestal

Game pâté on a pedestal

FOUR HOT ENTRÉES

A turban of pheasant à la Conti

Young chicken à la Régence

Game pâté à la royale

Rice casserole with a garnish of puréed game

FOUR COLD ENTRÉES

Eel galantine au beurre Montpellier

Fowl in jellied mayonnaise

Noix de veau spotted with jellied ham

Woodcock salmis in jelly

FOUR ROASTS

Young chicken in egg sauce

Teals garnished with lemon

Stuffed quails with bread sauce

Capons with egg sauce

FOUR GROSSES PIÈCES D'ENTREMETS

A Roman villa on a rocky outcrop

A Venetian fountain

An Irish pavilion on a bridge

A Persian pavilion on a rocky outcrop

FOUR ENTREMETS

Iced Génois in tiers

Iced tiaras in tiers

Meringues in tiers

French nougats in tiers

FOUR ENTREMETS OF VEGETABLES

Peas à la Parisiènne

Cauliflowers in mayonnaise

Green beans

Asparagus in butter

FOUR ENTREMETS OF MOULDS

Raspberry mousse

Orange jelly

Gooseberry jelly

Jellied 'liquer des îles'

In an age when descriptions of food are rarer than English truffles, there is one caustic account of this banquet, the sort of Carême meal the Stewarts claimed would 'never be forgotten in Vienna'. The diarist is an acid member of the embassy staff: the chaplain's wife.

Lady Stewart, a profusion of diamonds on her head and ten thousand pounds of pearls on her broad expanse of neck and shoulders... looked very splendid. Lord Stewart wore a full hussar uniform and yellow boots. The entire scene was theatrical... an awful, proud, dull assemblage of well-fancied head-dresses and well-flounced petticoats where one thought beyond rival rank or rival flounces never penetrates their phlegmatic carcasses.

And there we sat till supper was announced where my powers of description leave me in the lurch, but to say the supper was transcendently fine and the Germans are right good judges and right good stuffers. And so ends my story. The fête was superb and so well do Lord and Lady Stewart understand effect that they ought to have been managers of Drury Lane.

Antonin, of course, loved them. 'My life,' he said of his time with the theatrical couple in Vienna, 'had become beautiful!'

The Coronation of George IV was finally set for 19 July 1821, and Carême and the Stewarts set out to attend: he as chef, they as peers. It was a ceremony, and feast, that would go down in the royal annals for its unparalleled prodigality and chaos. Antonin and the Stewart party were delayed en route – despite the expedient of crossing on *Rob Roy*, the first cross-Channel steam packet (Antonin reproduced a sketch of *Rob Roy* in a later book, flying an unlikely French *tricolore*) and they arrived too late for the Coronation. Antonin nevertheless dined contentedly on the funeral-baked meats of his colleagues' reputations: 'I was happy not to have been there,' he said, 'from what I heard it was the saddest, shabbiest affair... which my former colleagues from Carlton House had utterly miscarried.'

Such extreme bitchiness was uncharacteristic of Carême but he had reason to be ungenerous. His former colleagues at Brighton – Benoit, Wilmet and Fournier – who had led the whispering campaign against him, were all recorded as having claimed vast expenses for their extra work, even taking coaches back and forth from Westminster to Covent Garden where the Coronation confectionery was being prepared. Their reputations never recovered from the ensuing fiasco at Westminster Hall.

As if things weren't bad enough at the farcical Coronation during which Queen Caroline had been forcibly barred from entering the Abbey, things went rapidly downhill at the banquet. The guests were unable to get at the food until the King retired, so the confectionery all melted, and the 3,903 different dishes were crushed in the mad rush to eat.

This was all particularly painful to Antonin – who had organised much larger affairs in France – because only half the

£276,476 bill for the disastrous Coronation feast was paid by the British Parliament. The rest was demanded from French taxpayers like himself – as war reparations following the defeat of Napoleon. He went straight back to Paris.

MACKEREL À LA STEWART

Boil trimmed mackerels in salted water. Serve surrounded by a ragout of mussels, crayfish tails and mushrooms. Garnish with mackerel roes, fried. In England they like the mackerel masked in a garniture of boiled gooseberries.

Antonin Carême

CHAPTER 13

Château Rothschild

After the decline of the nobility, money remains the only thing, and money without anxiety is the most beautiful of all beautiful things.

Henri Beyle Stendhal (1783–1842)

Carême's fame brought rewards but also challenges, and one of them was choice. Determining to resettle in France, he left the Stewarts but vacillated over the opportunities on offer. When in doubt, as so often before, he turned to freelance commissions for his *pièces montées.* His first was for an *extraordinaire* to celebrate the victory of the Bourbon Duke d'Angoulême in support of the Royalists in Spain.

In accepting this commission Carême aligned himself, perhaps unintentionally, with the reactionary 'Ultras', such as the old King Louis XVIII, and in opposition to his liberal protector Talleyrand. The work itself was a success: a feature comprising seven sugar-paste trophies grouped together, iced in imitation bronze and marble, and taking six weeks to complete. But the Duke de Grammont and the Duke de Périgord, 'Ultras' both, who inspected the work for the King's table, fell foul of Antonin's temper. They complimented the chef, and then asked what it had all cost. Antonin, affronted at the vulgarity of the question, replied grandly that the work was a 'homage' to the new France and his recompense should be whatever was felt appropriate. 'Some wounding observations were made,' he wrote – perhaps about his humble origins, or his new-found grandeur, 'and I decided to withdraw the work and send it for exhibition to the Conservatoire... the Restoration was not always great and gracious, nor was I the same young chef [I once was].'

Truculence is a not uncommon trait in chefs and Antonin, abandoned child of the rue du Bac, was ever on his guard for slights, real or imagined, from colleagues or from his social superiors. Cooking is an art in which the artist is undervalued and where dedication and long hours – Carême had worked six weeks without a break before this outburst – sit uncomfortably with service and civility to the ignorant. Like so many since, the haughty celebrity chef turned to more secure approbation: to writing.

Maître d'hôtel français, ou parallèle de la cuisine ancienne et moderne appeared in 1822 in five parts over two volumes. It is a unique conflation of cookbook and insights into royal catering, containing menus for every day of the year (based on his dinners at Valençay) while seeking to be both fashionable and reassuringly traditional. It covers the history of food and the dinners served to Tsar Alexander in Paris, to the Prince Regent in England and to Ambassador Stewart in Vienna, and includes everything from advice on buffets to discourses on, for example, turbot, 'the prince of all sea fish', which should 'never be served with Hollandaise sauce'.

At the time the book was sensational for its 'below stairs' insights into catering for the great gourmet-potentates of the day. This in turn gave a stamp of approval to Carême's elaborate precision of cooking and painstaking argument in favour of the new orthodoxy of *haute cuisine*. If it was good enough for the Brighton Prince of Pleasures and Alexander the Great, then it was good enough for every aspiring gastronome. Indeed Carême exhorted his readers to make practical use of his book. As he said, 'You can try this yourself at home.'

In *Maître d'hôtel* he balanced the needs of *service à la française* and *service à la russe*, stressing the presentation of food whether on plate or serving dish. Simply by leaving both possibilities open, he gave important endorsement to *service à la russe,* thus cannily pitching his book at the growing restaurant market, which invariably favoured plated courses kept warm with bell-like covers or *cloches*; Carême recommended padded leather ones, such as the Stewarts used in Vienna. He also began to codify the bewildering array of new foods and styles that were evolving into *haute cuisine*. For instance, he created the first genealogy of sauces, arguing that they all evolve from four classics: velouté, béchamel, Espagnol and

Allemande (thickened stock, thickened milk, thickened dark stock with tomato and egg/acid emulsions like Hollandaise). In his dedication he signed himself in almost aristocratic style as simply 'Carême de Paris'. By 1822, there was no better recommendation.

Now enjoying 'an Olympian fame', Antonin continued to be introduced to potential employers by his mentor, old Talleyrand. But he turned down offers of work from Lord Stairs, an English aristocrat in Paris, with a large fortune and a larger desire to establish himself in French society; as well as from Prince Esterhazy, the Austrian ambassador – rich enough to wear £80,000 worth of jewels at the recent Coronation in London; and from the Russian ambassador to Naples. Antonin cited the insufficiency of supporting personnel at his disposal in these households.

At the same time the new British ambassador to Paris, Lord Granville, a 'Leviathan of wealth', having struck rich with the Bridgewater Canal, effected an introduction via Talleyrand and offered Carême terms. Known in Paris as '*Le Wellington des joueurs*' for his notorious addiction to gambling, Granville once lost £23,000 in a single night. But even he, said Antonin, wasn't rich enough to lure him away from his writing.

The couple who finally tempted Carême out of his de facto retirement in 1823 had wealth to dwarf even a Leviathan like Granville. Their rise to affluence was perhaps unprecedented in France and was symbolic of the new bourgeois society buying Carême's books in 1820s Paris. They were Jewish first-generation immigrants and bankers and their name, little-known in France till after Carême joined their household, was Rothschild. Snob though he was, Carême did not hold their lack of aristocratic lineage against them. As he said, 'If the *nouveau-riche* man shares the good-life with his friends at table, he finds nobility of character and his soul is happy.' In this important sense the Rothschilds were truly noble.

James de Rothschild's estimated personal wealth in 1820 was 120,000 francs. It was 20 million by 1830 and 150 million in 1868. This is difficult to fathom in today's terms except relatively. In 1820 a Parisian labourer might earn 450 francs a year, of which 370 would go on bread. By the late 1820s when Antonin left his service, James was thousands of times richer than most Frenchmen and richer than any single man in France – even the King – by a factor of about ten.

1823 was a big year for Jacob de Rothschild (1792–1868) – known in France as James – the youngest of the Rothschild brothers who had set out from Frankfurt to dominate European banking. Aged 31, and only seven years after setting up the Paris branch of the family business, he became banker to the French government. He also, finally, became engaged – to his teenage niece. And he contracted Carême. The events were linked.

James had not at first been accepted in society. Before the 1820s he had been known at the Bourse and at the Longchamps racecourse, but not in the best boxes at the Opéra or at the salons of the Bourbon or Napoleonic aristocracy along the

Faubourg Saint Germain – for all he was their banker. The Rothschilds had come to prominence in French politics as bankers to the powers arraigned against Napoleon – it was their bank drafts that paid the allied troops on campaign. As reward, James became banker to the restored Louis XVIII. At the same time he bought No. 19 rue Laffitte, the former home of the Queen of Holland, Joséphine's daughter, Hortense Bonaparte. But his social stock still did not rise.

Part of the problem may have been that the Rothschild family respected wealth and achievement, even, one might say, celebrity, more than they respected the grandees of Paris. One story tells of a prince visiting Rothschild about a loan. The banker said 'Take a chair,' without looking up from his papers. 'Don't you know who I am?' said the prince. Rothschild shrugged, and, still not looking up, quipped: 'Take two.' But a more serious problem was anti-Semitism, even among those who accepted James's hospitality. In 1820, the Comte de Flahaut had written that dinner *chez* James was 'execrable and smelt of the synagogue'. Another guest, the Austrian ambassador, opined that James de Rothschild 'is small, ugly and arrogant. He gives parties and dinners but the great lords mock him.' Two things were about to change all that: Carême and Madame de Rothschild.

Betty de Rothschild (1805–1886), who has maintained a posthumous fame in Ingres's opulent portrait, was 19 when she married her uncle. She had been brought up in Frankfurt, Vienna and Paris, and was by any standards very polished.

Nevertheless, her engagement to the least prepossessing of the Rothschilds – her father's brother – caused little shock among her contemporaries. The Rothschilds had set out to be 'the richest men in Europe', and their schema included keeping the money in the family. Twelve of James's 13 nephews and nieces married first cousins. Betty further limited the gene pool by her marriage with her uncle – they had five children, four of whom married cousins. And yet, miraculously, theirs seems to have been a love match.

More valuable even than the 1.5 million francs dowry she brought to her uncle in marriage, Betty was a connoisseur of all the arts, especially music and food. Her expensive upbringing also gave her, according to one of her guests, the essential quality of an aspiring leader of high society: 'that noble indifference which gives the most sumptuous luxury the air of everyday habit'.

Carême was introduced to James and Betty de Rothschild by Prince de Rohan and was engaged as *chef de cuisine* for an annual salary of 8,000 francs. The money was only part of the incentive: Antonin undertook to give the Rothschilds 'the best table in Europe' but with substantial paid time out, to write.

Together, Betty and James planned an almost military campaign to win over the new post-Napoleonic high society. It was a campaign built on Carême's food. When Antonin first knew the Rothschilds in 1823, their townhouse on the rue Laffitte was being remodelled. The dining-room walls were painted as backdrops for Carême's *mises-en-scènes* with red distemper and classical figures, inspired by new drawings of the recent archaeological digs at Pompeii and Herculaneum. A 'Gothic-Renaissance' ballroom was constructed in the garden for Carême's larger banquets. Illuminated by chandeliers and with a stage large enough for a 40-strong orchestra, it could accommodate 3,000 guests. The whole scene was said to be a carnival of swags and garlands. A staircase that descended from the house into the ballroom boasted on each step a rare plant, a real Etruscan vase, an automaton, all in addition to a servant in black uniform and gold epaulettes. And at the bottom of the staircase was the place reserved for the centrepiece of Betty's balls and soirées: the Carême buffet. As the poet Heinrich Heine wrote, Carême's reign at rue Laffitte came to 'unite everything which the spirit of the 16th century could conceive and the money of the 19th century could pay for'.

The Rothschilds held gala after gala – an average week for Carême involved four major soirées, while dinner was never set for less than 12. Often lunch for 30 was followed by dinner for 60. Not even births or deaths in the family would interfere with the Rothschilds' determined entertaining. Carême cooked for 18 guests the night before Betty's first child, Charlotte, was born on 8 May 1825, while 26 were at dinner on the evening after the event. On the largest occasions Betty might borrow silver and servants from her father Salomon, whose mansion was only minutes away on the rue Pillet-Will, but this was rarely necessary. Records from her estate include one dinner service of 129 matching dinner plates and 113 dessert plates. They also include 2,666 bottles of Château Lafite in the cellars of the Paris townhouse alone.

With Carême at the helm, the Rothschilds gradually achieved acceptance, even ascendancy, within the new bourgeois high society. The best food, like the best art, could be bought, and the Rothschilds impressed Paris with their knowledge and acquisition of both. In the Rothschild letters details of finance, fame and food are liberally intermingled, whether in English, French, German, or their preferred Judendeutsch; everything from requests to send 36 pineapples to a country château, along with financial documents, to talk of a new Paris under-chef known as 'Le Petit Carême'.

Antonin's old friends Lord and Lady Stewart were guests at the rue Laffitte, and wrote jokingly that they were so impressed with Carême's new team that they were going to poach each trainee in the kitchen with a £50 bribe. Prince Esterhazy was entertained to 'a feast for epicures'; others to 'famous good dinners'; and even little Charlotte de Rothschild, aged only four, was politely writing back from the country 'with ten thousand kisses' in thanks for a gift of Carême's 'nice cakes'.

Yet the scale of entertaining in Paris was only part of Betty's and James's campaign for dominance of Parisian society, and only part of their impact on Carême's ever-growing fame. The Rothschilds were also adept managers of their wider public image and invited awestruck press reporters to their family weddings in Paris and London. *La Gazette de France* and *La Quotidienne* both covered Carême soirées in Paris in a style of prurient fascination – with fame, riches and glamour – that is more associated with our own age than with theirs.

Partly out of inherent artistic interest and partly with an eye on what would be said of her, Betty courted other celebrities along with her chef. Victor Hugo was a frequent guest at rue Laffitte, along with Honoré de Balzac, who modelled *La Maison Nucigen* on La Maison Rothschild. The society portraitist Jean Auguste Dominique Ingres knew Betty well, as did Paul Delaroche, Eugène Lami and Joseph Paxton, architect of the Crystal Palace, who would later help to build and decorate the new Rothschild château at Ferrières, where Carême was offered a country retreat. Chopin frequently played after Carême's dinner had been cleared, and Liszt wrote that he was inspired to new forms of melodic expression on hearing Paganini's violin after a Carême meal *chez* Rothschild. Rossini, who dedicated operas to Betty and Charlotte, was once asked at the Rothschilds' on what conditions he would tour America. 'Only if Carême comes with me,' was the response.

As a result of Carême's food, by the late 1820s the Rothschilds were 'the best the court and city offered in the way of distinguished society', and their poet-friend Heinrich Heine soon acknowledged that 'all Society now meets at their parties'. When King George IV in London was told that 'Chez Monsieur Rothschild ... one finds today the best table in Paris,' the fat king sighed and said, 'I can believe it, because Carême reigns over it.'

Betty's plan had worked. Antonin had created for her the finest soirées in Paris, if at a price 'beyond what any sovereign in Europe might be able to pay'. At the same time, the Rothschilds had given their chef more than just financial security and the freedom and secretarial back-up to write at an ever-increasing pace. In the sense that his name was mentioned in papers, periodicals and gossip-sheets in connection with the great artists and musicians of the age, they had made Carême a modern celebrity.

When the Rothschilds invited the famous lady of letters Lady Morgan to dine with them at Boulogne, they knew she would write about it. Carême knew it, too: if Lady Morgan sold her new book, *France in 1829*, on the back of his fame, he was happy to have her added endorsement in the English-speaking market. Or, in their own terms, Carême knew Lady Morgan could play Madame de Sevigné to his Vatel.

Clearly, Lady Morgan had a precursive understanding of the importance of writing about *food* if you are going to write about *France*: her mouthful by mouthful description of the dinner on the night of 6 June 1829 is unparalleled in the history of food-writing of this period. She also furnishes us with our only glimpse into Antonin's lifestyle at the height of his fame. According to Lady Morgan, the rue du Bac urchin now had a Paris townhouse, his own coach and his own box at the Paris Opera:

> To do justice to the science and research of a dinner so served would require a knowledge of the art equal to that which produced it. Its character, however, was that it was in season, that it was up to its time, that it was in the spirit of the age, that there was no *perruque* [fakery] in its composition, no trace of the wisdom of our ancestors in a single dish; no high spiced sauces, no dark brown gravies, no flavour of cayenne and allspice, no tincture of catsup and walnut pickle, no visible agency of those vulgar elements of cooking of the good old times... Distillations of the most delicate viands extracted in 'silver dews' with chemical precision 'on tepid clouds of rising steam' formed the *fond* of all. Every meat presented in its own natural aroma; every vegetable its own shade of verdure. The mayonese [sic] was fried in ice... and the tempered chill of the *plombière* (which held the place of the eternal fondu and *soufflés* of our English tables) anticipated the strongest shock, and broke it, of the exquisite avalanche, which, with the hue and odour of fresh gathered nectarines, satisfied every sense and dissipated every coarser flavour ... If crowns were distributed to cooks as to actors... [one] should have graced the brow of Carême for this specimen of the intellectual perfection of an art, the standard and gauge of modern civilisation!

SOUFFLÉ À LA ROTHSCHILD

Danziger Goldwasser is a liqueur containing suspended particles of real gold.

Soak five ounces of crystallised fruit in seven tablespoons of Danziger Goldwasser. Beat together seven ounces of pounded sugar with four egg yolks, then add three ounces of flour and two glasses of boiling milk. Bring back almost to the boil, but remove to add two whole eggs, the crystallised fruit and liqueur, and fold all into six stiffly beaten egg whites. Bake, in sugared soufflé dishes, or croustades with paper, for 25 minutes. Dust with pounded sugar five minutes before serving.

Antonin Carême

CHAPTER 14

Last Orders

*Burned out by the fire of his genius and the
charcoal of the rotisserie.*

Laurent Tailhade, *Petit Breviaire de la gourmandise*, on Carême

B y 1829, as the Rothschilds and Lady Morgan knew, Antonin Carême was unwell. Like the chef Vatel, wrote Lady Morgan, Carême would 'die *au champ d'Honneur* [from] great mental anxiety and great bodily fatigue'. Betty and James offered him land on which to retire at their new château at Ferrières, which Antonin graciously declined. He may have taken part in the planning of the kitchens, connected to the château by underground railway, but he left the Rothschilds completely in 1830.

'My prayer is not to end my days in a château,' the boy from the rue du Bac told the banker, 'but in my humble lodgings in Paris.' His 'humble' last abode at 37, rue Neuve Saint Roch, now a nursery school, is, however, hardly a garret. It has five elegant storeys and a coach entrance.

For one last time, George IV tried to lure Carême back to London. He sent Lord Conyngham – the epicene husband of the king's 'Fair Fat and Fiftyish' mistress – with a £500 contract sweetener and an offer of £4,000 a year plus stocks. Antonin's polite refusal was met with an offer to pay even more in advance, in case Carême was worried the obese King might die before the chef even reached the kitchens of the new palace being fashioned out of Buckingham House. Carême continued to refuse, and maybe just as well. In May 1830, George IV, 'The Grand Entertainment', finally lost his appetite and died, to few regrets – save maybe Antonin's – and to no one's surprise, of 'fat on the heart'. When questioned by Lady Morgan about his reputed disdain for the British royal household and its *'ménage bourgeois'*, Antonin tactfully avoided mention of his hatred for the Brighton chefs. He replied simply, 'My soul is utterly French and I cannot live except in France.'

Anyway, Antonin, too, feared that he was dying, and spent his last years in a fever of writing and publishing. In 1828 *Le Cuisinier parisien* was published, with 405 pages of his recipes and illustrations; there were also third and fourth editions of *Le Pâtissier royal parisien* and *Le Pâtissier pittoresque*. But throughout the late 1820s and into his full 'retirement' from the Rothschilds after 1830, Antonin devoted his energies to the masterwork he dedicated to Betty de Rothschild and Lady Morgan: *L'Art de la cuisine français au 19ème siècle*. Spanning eventually five thick volumes *L'Art de la cuisine* is Carême's lasting contribution to cookery writing: an encyclopaedia of thousands of recipes and the complete 'How to' of *haute cuisine*. It is scholarly in intent, including chapters on the history of food as well as more esoteric essays on, for instance, the 1825 Coronation banquet in the Kremlin and Napoleon's eating habits in exile. His style remains at once pedantic, and at times frustratingly vague – 'arrange with aspic and pigeons' eggs'. Still, nothing quite like it had been done before, and certainly not by anyone of Carême's celebrity.

By 1832 Carême was earning 20,000 francs annually in royalties from his collected works. With this money he engaged expensive doctors and a secretary, Frederick Fayot, to help him. He also worked in collusion with a Monsieur Plumerey, chef to Count Pahlen, the erstwhile Russian conspirator and omelette-maker. Plumerey would eventually complete the last two volumes of *L'Art de la cuisine* from Carême's notes.

Antonin's doctors thought he was suffering from intestinal tuberculosis, acquired from unpasteurised milk. In its final stages this would have been agonising – yet it was not his only, or his major, illness. His incremental weakening over the last years of his life and his final stroke-like paralysis suggest a different, additional, diagnosis. Carême was much more likely to have been suffering the effects of occupational low-level carbon-monoxide poisoning after a lifetime cooking over charcoal in confined spaces.

As his health declined throughout 1832 and he rushed to finish *L'Art de la cuisine* by dictation, for one last time Antonin saw an invader take Paris. Not the Russians on this occasion, but cholera. The pandemic swept from India via eastern Europe and hit London and Paris in 1832. By April, 1,200 Parisians were dying every day, only to be 'heaped up pell-mell', according to Georges Sand, in the 'absence of relatives and friends'. Just such a lonely, plague-shrouded burial was also to be Antonin's fate.

Mad rumours abounded that cholera was an invention of the Rothschilds and the new bourgeoisie to rid the cities of the urban poor. In an echo of the hysteria Carême had endured in the 1790s, one gastronome was murdered for the 'crime' of looking at the rich pickings in a pâtisserie window. Betty de Rothschild instructed that Carême's nourishing soups be distributed to the poor from Antonin's former kitchens at the rue Laffitte townhouse but she did not venture into Paris herself to visit the dying chef, for fear of cholera and mob violence.

Throughout the winter of 1832 to 1833, Antonin stayed in his grand house on the rue Neuve Saint Roch attended by his doctors, Fayot the secretary and a small group of visitors. His daughter Marie – who had been brought up in Paris while her father worked in England, Russia and Austria – came to live with him, taking dictation, and helping to nurse the parent she can barely have known as a girl. Pushed by his daughter and secretary in a bath-chair, Carême ventured out one last time – when the plague appeared to be abating – and expressed pleasure that, despite everything, so many fine pâtisseries were still in business. 'Nothing like it existed before me,' he said 'and my books.'

He sat reminiscing with Riquette, his old friend from the kitchens of the Elysée-Napoléon and St Petersburg. Young Monsieur Jay – his sous-chef in later years, and as such the man who perhaps knew Antonin best – was also a frequent visitor. And, despite the epidemic, various '*gens des lettres, gens du monde*' came to pay their respects, including an expert on the new science of food-canning who was anxious to discuss methods of preservation. Antonin remained mentally agile to the end, even arguing about the medicinal properties of mushroom soup with his physician, Dr Roque.

As evening fell on 12 January 1833, Carême became paralysed down the left side of his body, and for a while lost consciousness. Marie was with him, and Fayot, who described the scene. Towards the end of the evening, Antonin came to. Jay asked to speak to him, on 'sad and difficult' questions, according to Fayot. Antonin, recognising his intended son-in-law's voice, opened his eyes.

'Oh, it's you,' he said, 'Thank you. My good friend…' Jay must have wondered if there might be some last-minute resolution to the enormous emotional and financial questions that hung in the balance: his feelings for Carême's daughter, Marie; and whether he would be granted permission to complete *L'Art de la cuisine* without Carême. But Antonin continued in typical form: 'Tomorrow, bring me some fish. Yesterday the quenelles of sole were very good, but your fish was not right, you hadn't seasoned it well. Listen...' and with a feeble but clear voice he went on to explain how he wanted the fish cooked, demonstrating a movement with his right hand on the hangings of his bed by his side. He didn't speak again or recognise anyone. Half an hour later he died.

Carême's other doctor, Broussais, a disciple of the fashionable new 'science' of phrenology, took a cast of Antonin's head to study the areas of the brain supposedly responsible for culinary genius. Then the body was taken, under cover of night, to the cholera-choked new cemetery at Montmartre.

For many years no one even knew where the first celebrity chef was buried. No family or friends attended his lime-splashed obsequies in the chaos of the continuing epidemic, and his daughter, in the acrid aftershock of her bereavement, did not mark her father's grave.

Little is known of Marie, the famous chef's only child. But her figure casts a sad shadow over the end of Carême's short life, as much for what we must conjecture from her actions as for the little that we know for certain. No letters or personal effects survive from Antonin Carême. The only testament from this compulsive writer are his cookbooks – and one single letter.

It is a letter he wrote to his sous-chef, Jay, who was leaving Paris to open a restaurant-café in Rouen. The letter concerns Marie and her marriage to Monsieur Jay. Presumably all other correspondence – the letters from Tsar Alexander, Lord Stewart, the chefs Muller and Riquette, from Henriette Sophie and Agathe – were destroyed by Marie. The surviving letter hints at why:

Paris, le 10 décembre 1832

My dear Jay,

Since our last interview I have thought of nothing but you, and Marie, about our future and my failing health … but… why have you hardly replied with your reflections on our unhappy and touching interview? It seems to me, my good friend, you could write me a letter to inform me of your decision on the dear subject of our interview. Bear in mind that for a father the happiness of his child is the only hope that he holds dear in the face of a cruel illness. And so I repeat here and now… my dear Marie has good qualities, not only by instruction, she has a good heart, sensible and generous. She is used to wise economy, she does not have frivolous tastes because ever since she has been able to understand me I have taught her the self-sufficiency as I have had to practise through the horrible events of my poor life…

And so my dear Jay you know now that my heart and hopes are for your future happiness and that of my dear child, may time not ruin my hopes, and, if God permits my recovery as my doctors allow me to hope, we will be able to enjoy together days of peace and prosperity, and finish together my works which will dignify our profession and our future; our two hands, Jay, if you desire it as I do, will be forever inseparable.

I already have four new volumes ready to publish, my drawings are completed, I am going to get them printed and this new publication will double our income… If we can finish [the rest] we can confidently expect a revenue [from this] of 12,000 francs a year. You know well, my dear Jay, that you could finish this work if God calls me from this world and my dear daughter and her family can enjoy that which I have worked so hard for. Know well, my dear Jay, that I write from the bottom of my heart, that I have always thought that you could be, my dear friend, happy with [Marie]. Now it is up to you to let me know the result of your careful consideration on this great matter over the future name and dignity of Carême. My best regards to you and yours.

Your affectionate friend,

Antonin Carême de Paris

Carême wanted Jay as his son-in-law and heir. But something held Jay back. Some question over Jay's love for his master's daughter, over the Carême patrimony – the half-finished *L'Art de la cuisine*, the Paris townhouse or Marie's dowry – hung in the balance as life slipped from Antonin Carême.

In the light of this letter and of Marie's subsequent actions, a bleak conclusion seems unavoidable. Antonin had been arranging a marriage for Marie with a man who did not love her, and in her eyes a father's concern was mixed with the imperatives of preserving fame, fortune and an unfinished masterwork.

Marie and Jay did not marry. After Antonin's death, Marie thus found herself bereft of a fiancé as well as a father, and on the prospects of one and the memory of the other, she exorcised her distress and anger. She dissipated her father's effects, letters and fortune, took no interest in his fame or his grave, and prevented Jay from working on the concluding volumes of *L'Art de la cuisine*. She wrote only once about her father, claiming he had had 'insufficient interest' in money and cared only for the glory of his art.

Jay did indeed go on to be one of the most celebrated chefs of his generation. He ran a restaurant in Rouen which, after the coming of the railway, became an attraction in itself. Of Marie's subsequent life we know little. She did marry, however, four years after her father's death and the split from Jay. Her husband's name was Lanceroy, and he came from Étrépagny. He was not a chef. It seems they moved to Chârtres.

Perhaps the trauma that scarred Marie's bereavement was as simple and as powerful as a terrible jealousy of the love that her father had lavished on his books and his kitchens – and, by extension, his young disciple Jay.

Or perhaps she really had adored Jay and the pangs of her rejected love rebounded on the memory of her father. Antonin had been abandoned as a child, and in turn spent much of Marie's childhood pursuing his career far from Paris. Clearly, the international 'Father of the Great Chefs' was not entirely comfortable as a father to his own daughter. His botched attempt at arranging her happiness in tune with his own wishes seems to have been the final blunder in a relationship that never set, and at last turned sour.

In 1839 Marie's mother Agathe died too, at a small house on the rue Gaillon. According to Carême's (later) tombstone Agathe was buried with him, but the archives of the cemetery disagree. These suggest a place was reserved for Henriette Sophie, widow '*en première nôces*' of Carême and widow also, from a second marriage, to Antoine Michel Guyet, the witness at her earlier wedding to Antonin. She died aged 68, appropriately enough, on the rue Pot-de-Fer.

Talleyrand also lived to a grand old age. After an ambassadorship to the Court of St James's, he was buried at Valençay in 1838. As the ambassador in London he had been so appalled by the food at his London club, the Travellers' on Pall Mall, that he had had its chef, John Porter, study Carême, and in due course Porter had published the first English translations of Antonin's books.

EAU DE POULET RAFRAICHISSANT

Chicken Tea, for the unwell

Add two pints of water to an eviscerated chicken in a newly tinned stew pot. Boil for ten minutes with a pinch of salt. Add the yellow leaves of a lettuce. Boil it a further ten minutes. Add a handful of sorrel, chervil and beetroot leaves, cover and remove from the flame. After quarter of hour, strain it through a silk sieve and skim each cup that you serve.

Antonin Carême

Epilogue

He is for us a symbol. The father of modern cooking,
he also personifies the chef who lives only for his
profession, and is the prototype of the kitchen worker
who starts at the very bottom but by sheer force of
will and courage and — in his case — marvellous
intelligence, climbs to the very peak of his art.

La Vie professionnelle de Carême, Phileas Gilbert, chef

aris 1894. When the master pâtissier Charles Wallet
went in search of Antonin's grave 60 years after
Carême's death, he was shocked to find it unmarked
and overgrown. Gastronomy had flourished in 19th-century
France and the Society of Paris Chefs was rich enough to
sponsor the renaming of a Paris street in honour of its hero,
Carême. But the society could not trace a descendant to attend.

Wallet was further shocked to find that the grave of his
hero, as was the way in the more crowded Paris cemeteries, was
on the point of being recycled, its 'rent' unpaid. The Society

of Paris Chefs supported by the Syndicate of Paris Restaurants and Lemonade-makers, the Society of Pâtissiers and the Union of Paris Sommeliers, along with the award-winning chefs called the Disciples of Antonin Carême (who gather in honour of his name to this day) clubbed together to buy a tombstone.

The view Charles Wallet would have had that afternoon from above Montmartre cemetery has not changed so very much. In 1894 the white basilica of Sacré-Coeur, raised in thanks for another 'liberation' of Paris, was being built on the top of the hill, and across Paris, Eiffel's temporary tower marking the centenary of the Revolution was proving an immutable tourist attraction. Carême himself would have been harder pushed to recognise the city of his birth. In the generation since his death Paris had changed almost beyond recognition. The Montmartre windmills that had milled the flour for Bailly's pâtisserie – the original 'Moulins Rouges' – had nearly all disappeared. Avenues shone out from Étoile and the triumphal arch that Carême had never seen completed; and, as dusk fell, new streetlights illuminated pavement-side restaurants as far as the eye could see. The original Hôtel de Ville where Carême had catered for Napoleon's wedding was no more, and further Rothschild millions had totally remodelled the banker's palace on the rue Laffitte where Carême had cooked for Parisian society (including his near neighbour in Montmartre's cemetery, Heinrich Heine).

What Antonin would have recognised was the food. In the restaurants and bistros for which Paris had become famous since the Revolution and in the chic dining-rooms around the Faubourg Saint-Honoré – just as in London, Vienna, St Petersburg or San Francisco – Carême's cookbooks were on every kitchen shelf. Of the trinity said to have founded modern cuisine in post-Revolutionary Paris – Brillat-Savarin, de la Reynière and Carême – only one cooked. And only one became truly famous. A culture where the chef, not the writer or the critic, becomes a celebrity is a culture where food, too, is in revolution.

-⟪⟨◆⟩⟫-

CARÊME IS NOT widely read today, even by professional chefs. His style is far from the breezy encouragement of the modern cookbook; he was fighting for respectability for his art and responding to very different demands on the professional cook. Even so, his recipes still dress the tables of French restaurants the world over, adapted and rearranged to suit changing tastes and fashions. Surprisingly, in their original form, these dishes can be quite straightforward to prepare. If, as Carême suggests, you 'try them yourself', you may find them a little bland, a little sweet – and some of them wildly extravagant for most 21st-century gourmets – but his ghost lingers in the simplest, purest sauces as much as over the elaborate window displays of Parisian pâtisseries.

Indeed the smells, tastes and rituals of his time live on in unexpected ways. By 1914 and the end of the era in the history of food that has been called the 'Century of Carême', the pre-eminence of French cuisine was accepted throughout the

Western world, as was *service à la russe*. Carême's codification of sauces was taken as gospel in the professional kitchen as were his commandments of military order and strict hygiene. His constitution of bouquet garni and his staples of the pâtisserie had become orthodoxies. His introduction into the mainstream of the soufflé, the vol-au-vent, the piped meringue and even the humble tomato was taken for granted. So too was his insistence on crisply cooked produce – even when elaborately dressed or preserved (and as pioneered in the Collection Antonin Carême that sold Appert's canning technology under Carême's name from the 1840s)… and in every kitchen chefs wore and still wear Carême's hat.

Vitally, Carême established the model of the great chef who passes on knowledge and experience in published form – and in some cases becomes rich and famous as a result. As he said to Rossini, when the composer asked if he improvised in his kitchen: 'Oh no, I change very little in the execution, everything I do is written down.' It was a boast that acknowledged a constituency beyond palace walls; a public who would never eat food cooked by the 'King of Cooks and Cook of Kings' himself – but who were fascinated by his recipes. The result has been a chain of apostolic delegation, a debt owed by each cook to his predecessors, from Carême through Soyer and Escoffier, Bocuse and even Beeton to the celebrity chefs – and also to the salivating cookbook readers – of today.

Afterword

Page to stage to screen: a short life in books and kitchens

Autumn 2024

It all started at the Royal Pavilion at Brighton, the fantastical palace on the Sussex coast. Built as a temple to gastronomy, decorated eccentrically in fashions ranging from East Asian to culturally appropriated 'Indian' to neoclassical and even French Empire styles, the palace also features, as part of the tour, a rare survivor from the early 19th century: a functioning kitchen. This, The King's Kitchen, was opened around 1817 for and by Carême, and possibly according to his designs and instructions. The king of chefs was also, as it happens, a frustrated architect. 'This is where the great Carême cooked,' the Pavilion guide intoned on my serendipitous first visit there a quarter of a century ago, 'and where he invented caramel which is named after him.' (Like much of the best of culinary lore, this turned out not to be true at all, and the guides, maybe disappointingly, no longer say it. This is a shame in its way as 'caramel' may be the easiest way for Anglophones to learn to pronounce Carême's name.)

This trip to Brighton and to Carême's kitchen changed my life – or rather did so because of what happened subsequently, and because of the story I found. I was there, en route to France, writing about Fanny Burney, the 18th-century novelist and playwright in whose comedy, *A Busy Day*, written in France in 1800, I was to act in the West End production. I'd sold some story to a newspaper about her, and about France, as a way to publicise the play and, frankly, get an underwritten holiday in France. I am a writer but also an actor, a screenwriter and producer but originally an historian, and I have long been fascinated by this period; the 'Long Eighteenth Century' and the cultural tropes to which it gave birth. I also love to cook. Indeed, now I come to think about it, around this same time I created a small Regency-style dinner in my flat in North London for the theatre director of the West End play to meet the Burney biographer, Kate Chisholm. I think I used a Carême recipe, without even knowing it was such. Yes, these were some of the origins of this twenty-year-old recipe... I went on south from Brighton and, whimsical and hungry, stopped off at the Château Valençay in the Loire, really for no better reason than needing a lunch break and rather admiring Valençay cheese (the pyramidal goat's cheese with ash covering; that one). I took a tour of the château. And, in the kitchens, the French guide intoned, with an awe out-ranking even her counterpart in Brighton, that this was where 'the great Carême' had cooked. The play opened in London. And closed. A little while later, in the vagabond ways of an actor and one who loves a history adventure, I found myself filming in Russia. At Peterhof and again at Pavlovsk at Tsarskoe Selo outside St Petersburg (the 'Versailles of the Romanovs'), the dour Russian guide took us out via what had been the kitchens – now gift stores – and my translator told me that this is where 'the great Carême had cooked' and 'learned to cook like a Russian'. Which wasn't quite true either. But there, I thought, there was a *story* – maybe a film even: a three-part structure, a chef's-eye view of the world of *War and Peace*. A chef who had cooked for Napoleon, for Regency High Society and for the Tsar of All the Russias, and who was rumoured to have been a spy. I wanted to know more. There was something there – a story, and a story told with food.

On my return to London, I went to the British Library to order up some books on Carême. There were none. There was nothing in the catalogue but his cookbooks; the original French editions and some later English translations. I ordered the cookbooks anyway, wondering if they might give clues to some elusive story. The books were and are exquisite; lavishly illustrated with intricate engravings which I later learned were drawn by Carême himself, and some of the cookbooks even had pull-out folded pages like old-fashioned maps that took up the whole research table, featuring table designs and settings and illustrations of extraordinary culinary follies: fallen temples, ships in sail, towering urns overflowing with sugar-paste flowers and fruits. Some of them, in the way of old cookbooks that have actually been used in a kitchen, were spotted with grease stains. Sometimes it is an image that begets a story, and those first images in the library of Carême's spectacular and theatrical food-displays *'pièces montées'* and *'extraordinaires'*, as he termed them, first inspired me to tell this story, as a book, but ideally also as drama.

But was there a 'life' to excavate or a character to be revealed behind these dazzling illustrations and bizarre foods? (Vol-au-vents of cockerel's testicles, anyone? Snail soup?) Fortunately, yes; because, along with these recipes, or more precisely his descriptions of food, Carême had scattered little anecdotes *'memoires et souvenirs'*. Antonin must have kept a sort of recipe collection all his life before he published, a little like my mother in my mind, if much more elaborate, and, frankly, more name-droppy, that described the food but also noted who was there and for what occasion. And thus I found the primary evidence of what would be my first book: the piece-meal evidence of anecdotes and stories and places attached to recipes. Lord Castlereagh loved mackerel with gooseberries (who knew?). The Prince Regent (everyone knew) had a sweet tooth, an inexhaustible appetite and a stomach held in place by a 'Bastille of Whalebone' corset, and Napoleon, well, he seemingly lived up to his reputation as the lone Frenchman unaffected by food at all. 'No meal should take longer to eat than it takes to make love to woman.' I'll leave that one out there. It's of doubtful provenance anyway.

A picnic on Highbury Fields

I think I must have mentioned all this to Kate Chisholm, the Fanny Burney biographer, just as the play was closing in the West End. And also to Erica Wagner, then-literary editor of *The Times* and long-time correspondent about, often, food. They suggested I pitch Carême's story not just to film companies but also to Short Books, marketed then through Faber, and to Rebecca Nicholson and Aurea Carpenter, the then-publishers, and their talented designer Georgia Vaux and, as I recall, I did so over a picnic on Highbury Fields featuring some Carême pâtisserie and the vol-au-vents he 'created'. Short Books wanted unusual biography ideas: history from the sidelines or neglected stories of the past. Carême's tale was deemed perfect, a sort of antidote to classical literary biography because, even though Carême had been a bestselling author himself, he left little written record of his life or personality; rather it was his work and artistry that gave unexpected insights into a world shifting on its axis. It was a perspective from the kitchens and I think I also intended from the beginning a story told with and about food; an imaginative journey into a lost sensual universe. This is no less a concern for a historian than battles or kings; the lived reality of history was, of course, often about what was eaten. And with Carême there was a person-shaped keyhole into this lost world; the working conditions of the professional kitchen, just as gastronomy, the idea of a celebrity chef and restaurant culture itself were born. All this: and recipes.

And thus was born *Cooking for Kings: The Life of Antonin Carême, the First Celebrity Chef, A Biography with Recipes* as it was first titled (there was a vogue then for long titles. I think we played with *Carême* and *Caramel* and even *Napoleon's Wedding Cake*); a book which has never left me. By the time there were deadlines on copyedits, I was in a labour ward, distracting Claire, my partner, and myself from incipient parenthood by telling Carême's stories to midwives; my son Oscar about to be born. As the Irish say, babies bring their own luck, and the book was as well-received as any first time author has the right to wish for, and, under the guidance of my literary agent Ivan Mulcahy, it went on to a beautiful American edition and thence to many international translations, a lead feature in the *New York Times* Food Section and a CBS feature, Radio 4 Book of the Week, and became a documentary, 'Regency Banquet', about a day in the life of Carême at Brighton, and so on. I was a very lucky first-time biographer. It must have been baby Oscar.

Cooking for friends

Physical research has always been important to me, as both writer and actor. (I said this a lot at book events, until I came to write a biography of Casanova…) As historian, physical research – walking in the footsteps of, trying on the clothes even – can too easily be neglected, but if you are going to write about a chef, you need to know about cooking. Now,

I have worked in restaurants and as a (very bad) waiter. For Carême, I decided I needed to train as a pastry chef – for which I shall thank again the kind attentions and forgiving staff of *Pâtisserie Valerie*, then on Old Compton Street, Soho, and Eric Rousseau, the head pâtissier at *Belle Epoque* in North London. This, along with my long apprenticeship with my mother, currently stirring a gravy in front of me, turned out to stand me in good stead for a series of offers and opportunities in the wake of the original publication. First, I was asked to help recreate a Carême banquet at the Royal Pavilion, as part of a documentary on 'The Greatest Banquet ever cooked for a British Monarch'. Then, a request came to cook a Carême meal for the restaurant critic of *The Times*, and thence, and more alarming yet, after a mention of the book by Tom Stoppard and the actor Simon Russell Beale in a printed conversation, came a commission to adapt the 'day in the life of Carême' at the Brighton Pavilion as a stage play for Off-Broadway.

The dinner for food writer Giles Coren was alarming enough. A friend of a friend already, but a restaurant critic of fearsome, if witty, reputation, Coren was commissioned to review a meal, as cooked by me, and the book at the same time. I spent half a summer practising. Some of Carême's recipes are straightforward, some are indecipherable (who cooks with isinglass in the 21st century?), and some are merely drawings and a brief overview of composite parts. Of course, for the purposes of a story – which was always the point

– I chose recipes that combined a good story or visual flair. These, too, tended to dominate the menus I would cook from later on, both on television and on stage. Choux pastry swans, associated with Joséphine Bonaparte, featured along with a centrepiece; my best attempt at a *pâte-morte* (salt pastry) *extraordinaire*. A potage *à la Bagration*, which looks a treat if you can stand small crustaceans appearing to crawl out of a soup tureen, but that comes with an interesting story from Carême on one of the *grandes horizontales* of the First Empire. I think it was around this time that Ivan Day came into my life in a big way – Britain's leading food historian and the sort of enthusiast who will give advice and loan 18th-century jelly moulds at the drop of a hat, along with Mark Meltonville and Richard Fitch at Hampton Court Palace Kitchens who all became firm friends in the eccentric world of period-food. Thankfully, after my summer of rehearsals – partly in the kitchens of John and Danielle Lyons in France who suffered the failures that lead to victory – the meal was accounted a success, and *The Times* noted that Carême, the book and the story, was something of a drama. Soon after this was a call from Simon Green and Peter Tear, directors both, on the opening of a new theatre in New York, having read of Stoppard and Russell Beale's comments. They asked me to write and stage a one-man play about Carême… with live cooking. When in doubt about commissions (to misquote Carême): say 'yes'.

Dinner on the 59th Floor

I wrote the play as a day in the life of Carême at the Brighton Pavilion: his last day, the day Princess Charlotte of Wales died in childbirth, as a way to reflect on love and loss, on food and parenting. This structure remained in place from the documentary to even the first draft of the series' pilot, all of it based on the opening chapter of the book. I think I billed the play as a Restauration Comedy, but, in truth, as the lights went up and the audience were served tiny *petit fours* versions of the choux pastry swans 'Carême' had made on stage (thank you François Payard and chefs), what struck me were the tears. Carême's story could move people. Food accesses a particular part of our hearts and memories. The theatre smelled of vanilla and caramel for months after, they tell me, and they still served a Carême cocktail at the 59E59 Theatre bar.

The world of gastro-drama (I think it was Michael Batterbury of *Food Arts* Magazine who coined the term) has risen and fallen in New York most notably with whole turkeys deep-fried on stage, and whole vistas of family life and distant cultures played out with food. Sometimes, the audiences even get to eat. But the play affirmed for me a few simple issues as a dramatist. People remember stories where there is food attached. And audiences love also to smell and to eat. Of course, it was always going to be different on screen, for better or worse. Food dramas are rare, but they are landmarks of cinema: *Babette's Feast*; *The Cook, the Thief, His Wife and Her Lover*; *Big Night*; *The Taste of Things* – and more recently, via reality TV, television has woken to the potential of tales told in and around kitchens and the food industry: *Boiling Point*, *The Bear*. But Carême proved a challenging sell. Doors opened, in Hollywood, and closed. In London and eventually in Paris too … but the old truisms, that period-drama is too expensive a risk, doubled with the problems of recreating period-food and historic kitchens at work. At the end of the play's run, I was asked to cook a Carême meal for another documentary in the home of Elizabeth Kleinhans, the theatre owner, overlooking Central Park. The publishers came, and Ellen and Arthur Wagner, my landlords and friends, the theatre directors and, late from the ballet, Florence Fabricant of the *New York Times* Food Section and I was then asked what the future held, on screen, for this eccentric world of wonder that was Carême? The apparent enigma, at the centre of things that the biography could only hint at, was the question: What did Carême really want? To publish? To prove his craft an art? To find love and recognition through food? All pertinent issues to the drama of being Carême and unanswerable with the limitations of historical biography, but a journey of discovery for stage and screen. The play proved the necessary next step to dramatising Carême for film or television. Here was a man deeply damaged by his traumatic childhood, who appeared to have addictions – to applause, to sensuality, possibly to sex and other balms and stimulants – but who only had proper agency and animus in a story when a fictionalised emotional hinterland could be invented for him. And the essential enigmas: What happened in his private life and with his 'wives' and daughter, and what was his relationship with Talleyrand? These questions spurred on the creation eventually of my original pilot and TV series 'Bible'.

I often think, were it possible, an author would write a book *after* the book tour. Impossible of course, but it's only with a live audience you find out what people really want to know. Why was Carême important? How exactly did he change the way we eat? Can we ever know what foods tasted like at the time, or how ingredients performed under heat or in ice houses and with technologies now largely forgotten? Mark Meltonville, who worked with me on the *Richard & Judy* show series on food history and when *The Great British Bake Off* wanted a feature on Carême, and Ivan Day in Cumbria, taught me invaluable lessons on how we can only really know by making – like trying to understand Michelangelo by working out how to paint upside down. Carême was a scientist in this way, constantly experimenting, constantly wanting to push forward the technologies of his era while furthering his agenda of having the culinary crafts respected as Art. He was the Heston Blumenthal of his era, and he, indeed like this author, was experimenting with form and style. So, there are of course things I would do or say differently now. This was, after all, my first book, after which I went on to write a series of long and in-depth historical biographies, all of which profited from what I had learned whilst researching Carême. Short Books then had a policy of publishing without endnotes. There were originally many – it was closely researched – but that frustrates some readers as much of the narrative can seem speculative when, in point of fact, it is largely not. The opening chapter resorts to some surmise of what exactly Lady Morgan ate that day with the Rothschilds, and there is little direct evidence that Carême spent much if any time at Valençay, for instance. I was perhaps sometimes distracted by the glamour and eccentricity of the characters around Carême, and what one witty correspondent referred to as the 'name-drop soup' of his life story. But then again, that was some of Carême's magic: a sort of fame by association, and his story would have been utterly lost without it. But I note, rereading it now (a strange sensation a clear generation on, of revisiting one's younger self) that there was a singular problem with the use of evidence, but one that has stood me in good stead since. Sometimes the lack of a precise literary trail necessitates leaps of imagination and of empathy which I came to think of not as sins for the biographer at all, as the need to make informed speculations is exactly what allows access to seemingly hidden and neglected stories and insights into the past from neglected 'underclasses' like Carême's. The chapter on the Brighton years, for instance, was able to focus in intensely close detail on colleagues and payments and menus simply because the records existed (in Windsor and the National Archives in Kew) in ways the chapters just didn't for the Napoleonic years of Carême's career. This created an unexpected, or uneven, new style in the middle of the book depending really on your, the reader's, point of view. But you go where the evidence takes you, and the evidence cannot always be entirely literary or archival. The books I went on to write – on other lost or derided figures – all took me on similar journeys of eccentric detective work, and sometimes necessary speculation. I have Carême to thank for that. Culinary history, fashion history, sex history, medical history, servant, slave and backstage histories – all of these broad churches within which I have happily toiled, have in common the necessary reconstruction of a view, a wings-of-the-theatre perspective, if you will – of something that cannot be fully known or seen. Antonin taught me this. Learn by doing. Imagine by putting on the costume. Walk in their footsteps. Cook their food. Try to imagine the world as they may have seen it, smelled or tasted it. Read everything you can. Go everywhere. Then allow yourself to dream. Carême, as a result, also gifted me directly at least two of the subsequent books: *Beau Brummell, The Ultimate Dandy*, on the origins of men's tailoring, came out of the epigraph to the Brighton chapter. Casanova, too, I came to discover via Carême, had been rather more than the lover of legend but also an important food writer, giving me a new 'in' on him and his world of sensuality. And all of the books – Brummell, Casanova and a biography of the one-legged transvestite Samuel Foote – became dramas long before Carême reached the screen. Brummell, a BBC film; Foote, a West End play; Casanova, unexpectedly, but joyously, a ballet. And yet, Antonin – perhaps the best story I had come across to my way of thinking – fell at hurdles and on the long and winding road that is called 'development'.

For most of the first decade after the book was published and the Off-Broadway play was staged, there would be a call from my agent about twice a year of someone who had read the book and wanted to discuss it for the screen. There were exciting, well-oiled and mouth-watering lunches and dinners including a wild night with my late hero in food-writing, Anthony Bourdain, with Heston Blumenthal and Daniel Boulud and an approach from the representatives of the French movie star Romain Duris. Richard and Annie LaGravenese championed the story and encouraged me in my first proper pitches and pilots. There was even a book group, unusually of men, and more unusually in Hollywood, who read it and set about competitively bidding for it. It never quite happened. It turns out however that there *is* such a thing as a free lunch – at least if you've written about a chef. The project nudged forward, and would then falter. Too expensive. Too strange. Too French. Too sexy. Not sexy enough. And then there was a call from Paris from the producer Vanessa van Zuylen…

A five-hour lunch in Paris

I will skip forward. (That TV moment of 'here's one I made earlier'.) The course of development never does run smooth. I shall thank Siv Huor of Yungo Law, Paris, for all her work and diligence on my behalf, and the wise counsel of my dear friend

Jonathan Davies-Jones KC. Here we are. I will say, as I think I am allowed, that the initial five-hour lunch with Vanessa van Zuylen in Paris to discuss it all (and our life stories and thoughts on love and marriage and children as it happened) played out at Le Hibou on Carr de l'Odéon – yards from the site of one of Carême's iconic feasts – and was what convinced me at the time that Carême would be in safe and loving hands with her.

I wrote this book, twenty-one years ago, in order to forward a screen drama, and here we are.

Food for me is about family and friends. Carême lost the former twice, and seems to have had few close friends or colleagues, until perhaps his last years in the company of fellow 'celebrity' artists: Heinrich Heine and Gioachino Rossini. We can never know how things ended with Talleyrand, his professional godfather and perhaps more, nor can we truly know what went so catastrophically wrong in his relationship with his only child, Marie. In forging creative families around this story – or trying to – with publishers and publicists, with the theatre community and latterly with the television one – I wonder sometimes if I am trying to make amends for Antonin, or give him a happier afterlife. Of course, the essential question being answered in the stage play was: What happened at Brighton with Carême and his daughter? This is something we will never know. Likewise, really, the TV series was and is predicated on my unanswerable speculation in my pilot and treatment and TV 'Bible': What was the glue that kept Talleyrand and Carême stuck together for a lifetime? It may, of course, have been as simple as a shared love of food.

The first read-through of the pilot I wrote – it was then being developed in English – was with my Los Angeles writers' group: actors and screenwriters scattered over Zoom now between America and Europe – with the cast of a stage play I had recently been in, along with Richard Schiff as Talleyrand and Robin Weigert seducing young Carême as Joséphine. Even on Zoom, with no food and in a pandemic, it worked as it always had: as drama. It was, as it happened, my birthday – though I spent it alone for reasons not pertinent to this story except to say that Carême – and food – have kept me sane and comforted in times of bereavement and heartbreak as well as times of triumph. I ate a *tarte au citron* – more or less of his devising – as Carême's world unfurled again in front of me. Likewise, it being the pandemic, it was a meal alone on a *peniche* on the Seine when I first learned that the story was being taken up by Apple TV and thence into an adventure beyond my wildest imaginings…

Dessert. Location catering, French style

I turned up on location outside Paris, quite early in the shoot, a little after my son's twenty-first birthday and my daughter's eighteenth. To drive through the château gates and see a cast and crew of two hundred going about their focused business is quite a moment for any writer, but notably after this journey. Poignantly, I recall that that first day they were shooting a scene I had created quite early in the process of the screen and stage adaptations: the initial encounter between Carême and Talleyrand, imagined at the Hôtel de Galliffet on the Left Bank, but recreated in a private château north of Paris. A writer on set always feels a tad redundant. Some people are free to, or want to, talk. Most are focused on the task in hand: to push all those hours of preparation and storytelling, the work of so many departments, through a camera lens.

One end-point meal to this story – though there will be more – involved a glass of wine and several cigarettes that day (this being French location-catering) with Benjamin Voisin, our young Carême, who mined me for background on Antonin, asking for a signed copy of the book. As I did so, I reflected that Benjamin could not be much older than the 21 year-old biography I wrote – or than my son. This story of meals, Carême's and mine, it turns out, is very much about parenting: Jean Gilbert's, Talleyrand's – the tortured relationship of Carême and his 'wives' and daughter, and I hope, on screen as intended, some of the potency of the metaphor – a life spent cooking – underscores an epic but enigmatic life. Writing next about Casanova – who knew a thing or two about love and about food – I came across a lovely turn of phrase in French in the notes to his memoirs: that love, like cooking a meal with people you love, requires a 'mutual complicity of shared imagination'. It is one meaning of love and family for me, I reflect as I watch my mum, as I did as a small boy, cooking. It is one meaning of bringing a drama to the screen, and this story is now shared again, with a vast team of complicit or intended-complicit professionals, and with you. I hope that Carême – and his family, whoever they were – would smile.

CARÊME'S WEIGHTS
& MEASURES

Carême's career spanned the attempted introduction of the 1792 Revolutionary metric system to France. This system of grams and litres, centimetres and metres did not become legal until November 1801 and Carême never took to it. He published his recipes using the vernacular system of glasses, spoonfuls and even platefuls, as well as the older system based around *pintes* and *onces*.

Le gallon = 4.54 litres
La pinte = 0.931 litres
Le setier = half a *pinte*
Le demi-setier = quarter of a *pinte*
Le poisson = eighth of a *pinte*

In weight, he used ounces, or rather the pre-Revolutionary *once*, *livre* (pound) and the *quateron* (quarter-pound). Carême's *once* or ounce equalled a sixteenth part of a *livre* or pound as in modern British Imperial measures. This was only the case in Paris: the 'livre' varied in meaning throughout

France, between 300 and 552 grams, and though divisible in Paris (and by Carême) into 16 ounces, was made up of 12 ounces, for instance, in Lyons. Carême used also *pain de beurre* in his recipes – not unlike the way butter is sold in modern America. These pains were rolls making up about 4 ounces or 125 grams. He used *maniveau* or small wicker punnets as a measure of mushrooms, herbs and soft fruit.

His dram = 60 grains, or an eighth of an ounce

These recipes use the measures, and some of the translations, of the first English-language editions of Carême's works from the 1830s and 1840s by the Victorian chefs William Hall (chef to the Speaker of the House of Commons) and John Porter (chef at the Travellers' Club, Pall Mall).

CARÊME on SUGAR

Clarifying and the five degrees of boiling

Carême codified the stages of sugar boiling for different purposes in confectionery, culminating in caramel. Carême's terms and tests are used in pâtisseries to this day.

To clarify sugar:

After beating up the white of two eggs with two glasses of water till very frothy, add 15 glasses of water, stir the whole well together and put aside two glasses of this mixture. Add afterwards eight or nine pounds of fine loaf sugar, broken in small pieces, and then put your pan on a moderate fire. As soon as the syrup boils, put the pan on the corner of the stove and pour a fourth part of the water which you have preserved in it. Skim the syrup and as the scum rises to the top, add a little more of the water which you have put aside, until the sugar ceases to throw up any more scum, after which pass your syrup through a silk sieve, or napkin lightly wetted.

Of boiling sugar:

Fingers, dipped in iced water, can be used to test boiling sugar.

Au lisse – 1st degree:

After boiling a few moments the clarified sugar, take a little of it on the top of your forefinger and press against your thumb; when, on separating them immediately, the sugar forms a tiny thread hardly visible, but which you draw out a little, it is a sign that your sugar is boiled *au grand lisse*, but if on the contrary it breaks instantly, your sugar is only *au petit lisse*.

Au perle – to a pearl – 2nd degree:

After further boiling, again take some between your fingers which on separating them immediately will cause the sugar to extend like a string. When this string breaks, your sugar is called *au petit perle*, but if it extends from one finger to the other, without breaking, it is proof that your sugar is boiled *au grand perle.* The bubbles thrown up by the sugar in the latter case should, besides, appear on the surface like small close pearls.

Au soufflé – 3rd degree:

Continue boiling the sugar and then dip a skimming net in it which you strike immediately on the pan. Then blow through the skimmer, and if that causes small bubbles to pass through it, it is a sign that your sugar is boiled *au soufflé*.

À la plume – 4th degree:

Let the sugar boil again, then dip in the skimmer and shake it hard, in order to get off the sugar, which will immediately separate itself from it, and form a kind of flying flax. This is called *à la grande plume.*

Au cassé – to a crack – 5th degree:

After boiling the sugar a little longer, dip the end of your fingers in cold water, and then in sugar and immediately after in cold water, which will cause the sugar to come off the finger. If it breaks short, it is boiled *au cassé*, but if, on putting it to your teeth, it should stick to them, it is only boiled *au petit cassé*.

Au caramel – 6th degree:

When the sugar has been boiled to the 5th degree, it passes very quickly to a caramel; that is, it soon loses its whiteness and begins to be very lightly gold coloured, which proves that the sugar is boiled to a caramel.

༜

CARÊME'S four CLASSIC SAUCES

Talleyrand said that the British had three sauces and 360 religions whereas the French had three religions and 360 sauces, though the Compte de Croze counted more than 500. Carême claimed all these sauces could be put into four families; the four Classic Sauces, from which, he argued, all others are descended.

༜

SAUCE BÉCHAMEL
(named after the maître d'hôtel of Louis XIV, the Marquis de Béchameil 1630–1703)

half an ounce butter
2 tablespoons flour
half a pint milk
salt and pepper
grated nutmeg
1 shallot stuck with a clove
bouquet garni

Heat the butter and stir in the flour and add, gradually, the milk, shallot, nutmeg and bouquet garni. Simmer very slowly for 20 minutes, remove bouquet garni and shallot before serving.

SAUCE VELOUTÉ

1 ounce butter
1 ounce flour
3 glassfuls of stock – preferably veal
salt and pepper
pinch of nutmeg
pinch of ground ginger

Melt the butter and stir in the flour. Add gradually the stock, ginger, nutmeg and seasoning. Bring to the boil and simmer, skimming occasionally, until reduced to a half. The sauce should now be thick but light and creamy. Add cream to turn this into the white glaze sauce for chicken *à l'ivoire*.

SAUCE ALLEMANDE

1 ounce butter
1 ounce flour
half a pint boiling water
salt and pepper
1 egg
3 drops of wine vinegar

Melt the butter, add the flour and then the boiling water and seasoning. Off the heat, whisk well the egg and vinegar and add gradually to the sauce whilst whisking. Do not reboil.

SAUCE ESPAGNOL

2 ounces butter
1 ounce flour
1 pint dark meat stock
bouquet garni
1 ounce tomato purée

Melt the butter, stir in the flour and cook gently on a low heat until well browned. Add the stock and stir until it thickens. Add the bouquet garni and simmer half an hour. By this time the sauce will have reduced. Remove the bouquet garni, add the tomato purée and simmer another five minutes. Makes one pint.

Carême – and this recipe – were instrumental in bringing the tomato into the culinary mainstream.

SOUPS

—❦—

POTAGE À LA CONDÉ
Château Rothschild, 1829

Carême served this soup at the Brighton Pavilion, at Vertus and for the Rothschilds, Stewarts and Princess Bagration, often thinned down with stock (consommé of fowl). Vatel had been chef to the Prince de Condé, so any recipe dedicated to this famously gourmet household had the stamp of ancient lineage.

3 pints of red haricot beans – soaked overnight
1 partridge
1 medium (8 ounces) piece of lean ham
1 carrot, 1 turnip
2 leeks, trimmed
1 head of celery, trimmed
up to 4 pints prepared game, chicken or veal stock
bread to fry, for croutons

Wash three pints of red haricot beans. Place in large pot with a piece of lean ham, a gutted partridge, and a carrot, turnip, two leeks and a head of celery, all tied together. Cover with water and boil for three hours; remove the ham and tied roots,

244

rub through a sieve, add more consommé of fowl, let simmer for two hours to clarify and serve with fried bread.

POTAGE ANGLAIS DE POISSON À LADY MORGAN
Château Rothschild, 1829

Carême created this soup for Lady Morgan. Based on his classic fish soups, it was designed to impress. He published the recipe, with her name attached, in *L'Art de la cuisine française* (1833).

For the soup:
1 medium-sized brill
1 sole
1 eel
1 bottle champagne
1 lemon
2 medium onions, chopped
1 stick of celery, chopped
2 leeks, trimmed and chopped
half a bay leaf
2 anchovies, washed
thyme
basil
rosemary
marjoram
nutmeg   *Continued overleaf*

Cayenne pepper
cloves
salt
4 pints veal stock

For the garnishes:

1 lb truffles, peeled (reserve the trimmings)
2 dozen crayfish
2 dozen oysters
2 dozen button mushrooms
1 large whiting
1 lb unsalted butter
1 egg yolk
2 pints clear, light consommé

The soup:

Wash and fillet a medium-sized brill, a sole and a small eel. Reserve the flesh. Place the bones, heads etc., chopped, in a casserole with a bottle of champagne, the zest of one lemon, the peelings from a pound of truffles, two onions, a carrot, a celery stick and two leeks, all the vegetables chopped. Then add half a bay leaf, a small bundle consisting of thyme, basil, rosemary, marjoram and a pinch each of nutmeg and Cayenne pepper, two cloves, two well-washed anchovies and a little salt. Remove the bundle of herbs after an hour of simmering and pass all through a silk sieve. Dilute to taste with a good veal stock.

The garnishes:

Sauté the fish fillets and separate the flesh into small escalopes. Set aside, draining on serviettes. Meanwhile, poach two dozen crayfish, peel and reserve for garnish. Keep the shells.

Whiting quenelles:

Cook the filleted flesh of a large whiting in *beurre d'écrivisse* (butter clarified with crayfish shells). Once cold, add the yolk of an egg and form the quenelles of buttered fish between two coffee spoons, poach briefly in consommé and set aside. Keep the consommé.

Poach the peeled truffles in consommé. Slice the truffles with a *coupe-racine* (a little like a Chinese mandolin) into thumb slices the diameter of a thumb print. Keep the consommé.

Open two dozen oysters. Prepare 20 peeled white mushrooms, blanched in consommé. Add the consommés from cooking the quenelles, truffles and mushrooms to the potage. Bring to the boil, and clarify. Serve with quenelles, fish escalopes and mushrooms in the soup, and crayfish tails, truffles and oysters decorating the rim of the plate.

POTAGE OF PURÉED PEAS WITH SMALL CROUTONS
Château Valençay, 1806

3 quarts (6 pints) fresh garden peas
water to cover
bunch of parsley
dram of salt
quarter of a pint reduced game consommé
2 ounces unsalted butter
butter-fried croutons

Take three quarts of newly shelled peas, cover with water and boil with a bunch of parsley and a little salt. Strain – keeping the water – and remove the parsley. Place the peas in a basin with a consommé of game reduced to a demi-glaze (i.e., a reduced, strained, strong fowl stock). Strain through a sieve.

Just before serving, reboil the water but not the pea purée, add the two together at the last minute with a pat of butter in the middle. Serve the croutons separately.

❧

POTAGE DE BISQUE D'ÉCRIVISSES À LA RÉGENCE
Brighton Pavilion, 1817
Regency Shrimp Bisque

Carême added floating quenelles made from moulded pressed chicken breast as part of his regime for the Prince Regent and called it Potage Santé à la Régence. This original version is prettier.

For the soup:
50 small crayfish
6 ounces risotto rice
4 pints fish or veal stock
1 ounce butter
10 parsley stalks
1 medium onion, sliced
handful of mixed chopped marjoram and chervil

For the garnishes:

croutons of fried bread
half a pound unsalted butter (for crayfish butter – needs to
    be prepared the day before)

For the pain de volaille:

4 chicken breasts
pinch of nutmeg
2 spoonfuls of thick béchamel sauce
8 spoonfuls of chicken stock
8 egg yolks

For 15 according to Carême – modern soup plates tend to be
larger – these quantities will serve up to eight.

The soup:

Boil six ounces of risotto rice in stock until soft. Boil 50
small crayfish in two large spoonfuls of prepared consommé
(Carême advises fish stock in Lent or for dieting) with a nob of
butter, a pinch of pepper, parsley stalks, one sliced onion and a
small handful of chopped marjoram and chervil. The crayfish
will turn an attractive pink as they cook – less so if they are
bought with shells only on the tails, as it now common.

Remove the shells if such there are. Keep a dozen or more
of the better-looking crayfish for garnish, with tails attached
but flesh exposed. Strain the liquid off. Press the rest of the
meat with the cooked rice and strained juices through a sieve.

At this stage dilute to taste with a good stock (fish or veal)
About two pints will make a hearty soup, three something lighter.

The garnishes:

croutons of fried bread

the reserved crayfish

Crayfish butter:

Pour melted butter into a mould with discarded crayfish shells. Leave overnight. Reheat, and strain off the fish shells. Put back in the fridge overnight.

Pain de volaille (for the Potage Santé à la Régence):

Take four chicken breasts, sauté with salt, pepper and nutmeg (a pinch). Cut into small pieces, and add two spoonfuls of thick béchamel sauce, eight spoonfuls of a good chicken stock, and eight egg yolks.

Pass all through a sieve. Place in buttered mould in a bain-marie in a low oven for an hour and half. This solid block of formed chicken can then be cut into cubes or oblongs.

꩜

POTAGE BAGRATION
Hôtel Bagration, Paris, 1820

Princess Katerina Bagration, a famed beauty, had affairs with Metternich, Talleyrand and the Tsar. She battled constantly with her weight and when she employed Carême in Paris in 1819 he created a 'health' regime for her as he had for the Prince Regent. Unfortunately it reduced her to 'almost total inactivity' and he left her service.

For the soup:

2 sole – with heads
half a pint thick sauce velouté
1 *maniveau* small white mushrooms
3 pints veal stock
unsalted butter
cream

For the garnishes:

10 crayfish tails
2 sole for sole quenelles and fillets of sole
1 egg yolk
consommé for poaching

The soup:

Boil the whole soles and the mushrooms in enough water to cover for at least half an hour. Remove bones and press through a sieve. Dilute to taste with veal stock, and thicken with velouté.

Finish before serving with fresh butter and cream.

The garnishes:

Fry small crayfish in butter, keeping the shell on the tail and exposing the rest of the flesh. Steam two sole gently, only until the flesh sloughs from the bone. Remove onto a napkin. Preserve the most attractive small pieces of fillet. Press the rest of the flesh through a sieve, add the yolk of an egg, and work into a paste with a little *beurre d'écrivisse* (see Potage à la Régence). Mould between small silver coffee spoons and poach in consommé.

Serve with the quenelles and fillets floating in the soup, and the crayfish tails arranged on the plate rim.

FISH

LE BAR GRILLÉ À L'ITALIENNE
Château Rothschild, 1829
Grilled sea bass in an Italian champagne sauce

1 large sea bass
2 glasses champagne
2 glasses sauce Allemande (see above)
1 ounce butter
2 spoonfuls chopped mushrooms
1 shallot
1 clove *rocambole* garlic
juice of 1 lemon
thyme, rosemary, pepper, allspice

Bass: filleted and lightly grilled.

The sauce: sauce à l'Italienne au vin de champagne. In a sauce pan, place a glass of champagne, two spoonfuls of finely chopped mushrooms, a shallot, a clove of rocambole garlic, a little thyme and rosemary, a pinch of pepper and of allspice. Reduce, and remove the herbs, add next two glasses of sauce Allemande and reduce further on a very low heat. Add a further half-glass of champagne and place the sauce in a bain-marie. Just before serving, swirl in a knob of butter and the juice of one lemon.

CABILLAUD À LA HOLLANDAISE
British Embassy, Vienna, 1821
Cod à la Hollandaise

1 large cod
half a pound sea salt
3 pints of boiling water
1 pint milk
1 pound unsalted butter
4 lemons
pepper, salt, nutmeg
boiled potatoes and parsley to garnish

Cod: freshness should be checked, by the eye, which should be full and rising from the head, surrounded by a flaky substance, transparent and red. The gills too should be red. Salt generously inside and out and lay on ice.

Two hours before serving, remove the head and tie up the neck. Wash out the salt. Make six large incisions inclining towards the head. Lay belly down in boiling water, half covering. Add a pint of milk and allow to boil slowly.

When the flesh at the incisions starts to open, take it up and place on a napkin to drain. Surround with boiled potatoes, branches of parsley and serve with two sauce boats of simple butter sauce (butter, lemon juice – one lemon per sauce boat – pepper, salt and nutmeg).

৵৽৹

PETITS TRUITS AU BLEU
Château Valençay, 1806
Trout dipped in boiling water alive

Although 'au bleu' is often taken now to mean boiled alive, Carême's recipe is more humane; a bluish tinge is preserved in the colour of the fish by the vinegar in which it is marinated.

1 15-inch trout
2 12-inch trout
2 ounces sea salt
1 glass white wine vinegar
2 ounces unsalted butter
3 pints fish stock
pepper, salt
nutmeg

Take three trout, two 12 inches long, one 15 or more, so that the largest will fit in the middle in a tight fish pan. Remove the gills and innards, wash, drain and strew then with a little salt. Do not scale them. An hour later, wash, dry and tie them up, lay them in the fish kettle, and throw in a pinch of pepper, salt and grated nutmeg, and afterwards pour over them a little boiling vinegar. Add some fresh butter, and cover with a fish bouillon. Half an hour before serving, bring to the boil, and simmer for ten minutes. Remove from fire but leave them covered. Just before serving, remove from fish kettle and serve on napkins.

SALMON À LA ROTHSCHILD
19 rue Laffitte, Paris, 1825

This recipe requires four bottles of champagne, enough truffle shavings to cover a large salmon, not to mention mussels, smelts, crayfish tails and the patience to cover an entire fish with a paste made of another…

1 enormous salmon
4 bottles champagne
1 pound truffles, pared and sliced
20 small crayfish
1 pound steamed mussels
5 small soles
24 smelts
4 whiting
1 large loaf stale French bread
2 pints fish stock
6 ounces butter
1 tablespoon thick béchamel sauce
3 egg yolks
1 egg white
6 ounces best *mirepoix*

chervil, parsley, tarragon
salt, pepper, nutmeg
tarragon vinegar

For the stuffing and paste: four whiting – poached lightly.

Soak a large loaf of white bread in fish stock, for at least an hour. Squeeze out the excess moisture. For every six ounces of this bread '*panada*', add six ounces of butter, and ten ounces of flaked cooked whiting. Add a tablespoon of thick béchamel sauce, three egg yolks, two tablespoons of fine herbs (a mixture of chervil, parsley and tarragon), a little nutmeg and pound thoroughly. Pass all through a sieve and set aside.

Stuff a large salmon with the whiting forcemeat. Tie it up, and lay it on a fish strainer well-buttered. Mask the entire surface with the whiting forcemeat, an inch thick, and make it smooth by dipping a knife in warm water, then wet it with a brush dipped in egg white to fix upon the forcemeat some large half-moons of truffles in the form of the scales of fish, pressing them down lightly with the blade of a knife.

Put the salmon in a fish kettle with an excellent *mirepoix* moistened with four bottles of champagne – all passed through a sieve. The *mirepoix* should be quite well-seasoned.

When it boils, place buttered paper over it and set it in a medium oven – with heat from above and below – so that the boiling is only gentle, for two hours. Take it out, remove the strings, lay it on a large dish and surround it with a ragout of escalopes of fillets of sole à la Venitienne,* steamed crayfish tails and mussels.

Garnish the fish further with eight *hâtelets* (skewers) composed of fried smelts, and serve the champagne sauce, strained, in boats.

*SOLES À LA VENITIENNE
19 rue Laffitte, Paris, 1825

Soles boiled whole for 35 minutes in a sauce of butter, salt, pepper, nutmeg and tarragon vinegar.

PERCHE À LA HOLLANDAISE
Brighton Pavilion, 1817
Perch with Hollandaise sauce

5 large perch
1 whole lemon, sliced
1 onion, sliced
1 carrot, sliced
1 small bunch parlsey
1 pound butter, melted
juice of 4 lemons
boiled potatoes to garnish
thyme, bay leaf, mace
salt, pepper
nutmeg

The perch from rivers are better than those from ponds, the flesh being whiter, firm, flaky and of exquisite flavour, digesting with much facility and is of all the fish the most nourishing. The very large or the very small are not so good as those of middling size. When old, the flesh becomes tough and loses its fine qualities; when young the flesh is viscous. Nevertheless the larger ones are more sought after for purposes of the table. The freshness is known by the brilliancy of the eye and the red tint on the gills.

Have five large clean perch, and tie up their heads, boil them in salt and water with a lemon cut in slices, an onion and a carrot sliced, whole parsley, thyme, bay leaf, and a little mace.

Boil nearly half an hour. When done, take them up and lay them on a cloth, cut off their fins, and with a knife take off all the scales on both sides, then dish them with potatoes boiled in salt and water.

Stick upright the red fin of the perch down the centres of each fish, and serve with two boats of melted butter, to which add salt, pepper, lemon juice and a little grated nutmeg.

MEAT, GAME & SAVOURY PASTRIES

⬫⬫⬫

GIGOT DE BRETAGNE BRAISÉ
DE SEPT HEURES
Louvre, 1815
Leg of Breton lamb cooked for seven hours

Breton and Normandy lamb and mutton were considered the best. In demanding a *'gigot tendre'* Carême used when available the *présalé* lamb that grazed on salt marshes in Northern France.

1 leg of lamb
olive oil
Cognac
seasonal herbs to include rosemary
1 bottle white wine
1 pint veal stock
sauce Espagnol (see above)

Choose a tender leg of lamb and marinade it overnight with oil, Cognac, herbs and spices. Before cooking, sponge it dry and sear it in hot butter.

Place, quarter covered in white wine, bouillon and thickened velouté or sauce Espagnol (reduced by half) in a roasting dish, in the middle of a slack oven. Cook for seven hours, basting and turning frequently (Carême uses a turning spit over a basting tray). Slide on to a plate and serve garnished with braised and glazed vegetables and accompanied by the cooking juices, strained and skimmed of fat.

ᐧᑌᕊ

COLD SALMI OF PARTRIDGES
British Embassy, Vienna, 1821
A salmi is made from cooked game

6 partridges
1 large truffle, boiled in champagne
1 double cocks'-comb
half a bottle Hock white wine
half a bottle Burgundy white wine
1 bay leaf
4 shallots, peeled but whole
half a pint veal stock
half a pint sauce Espagnol (see above)
half a pint aspic jelly
boiled root vegetables for garnish

Roast six fine partridges, and when they are cold, take off the thighs, the wings and the breasts, remove the skin and trim them neatly. Wipe them with a napkin, and put them in a stewpan; put the bones and the trimmings in another stewpan, with half a pint of hock and the same of white burgundy, a bay leaf, and shallots. Cover and place the stewpan over a quick fire; when about half reduced, add a ladleful of veal stock and when boiling set the stewpan in the corner of the stove, to boil an hour.

Skim it carefully and strain through a napkin, replace it in a small stewpan over a large fire with two ladlefuls of clarified sauce Espagnol, stir with a wooden spoon to reduce quickly, and at the same time to prevent it burning. But to render it brilliant, leave it at intervals without stirring, adding at each time some spoonfuls of aspic jelly.

When reduced sufficiently, pass it into a smaller stewpan (it should be a little thick) and stir it from time to time with a spoon, that it may be very smooth as it cools. Then pour a fourth part over the pieces of partridge, which lay out on a baking sheet, to mask their surfaces.

When the sauce is cold, dish the thighs in a close circle, on which again lay in the same manner the ten fillets and on them four breasts and on those the remaining two, and crown the whole with a fine truffle boiled in champagne wine, and not peeled, and fix upon it a large double cocks'-comb, dressed very white.

Then work the sauce with the spoon, and if too thick, place for an instant on the fire, just to warm the stewpan only, but on the contrary if too thin, put it on ice which will immediately set it.

When fit to mask, it should quit the spoon with difficulty, forming a strong but very smooth cord, then carefully pour it over the salmi, removing the truffle, but replacing it again, and surround with a handsome border of roots or aspic.

෴

LES PETITS BÉCASSES TRUFFÉES
Palais de Luxembourg/Odéon Theatre, 1816
Hot snipe pie with truffles

This recipe may be adapted for lark, pheasant or quail

12 ounces plain flour
6 ounces butter
2 egg yolks
half an ounce salt
water
8 snipe
3 ounces melted butter
3 ounces grated bacon fat
1 tablespoon chopped parsley
2 tablespoons chopped mushrooms
4 tablespoons chopped truffles
1 small clove shallot (blanched and chopped)
4 tablespoons of forcemeat
2 tablespoons chopped sweet herbs
1 egg
sauce Espagnol, reduced (see above)
salt, pepper, nutmeg
laurel leaves

To make paste for hot pie:

Take three-quarters of a pound of sifted flour, six ounces of butter, the yolks of two eggs and two drams (120 grains or quarter of an ounce) of fine salt. Having put the flour on a board, make a hole in the centre and put therein the butter (to be worked in winter), the yolks of the eggs and the salt, together with a quarter of a glass of water. In summer be sure to use iced water, and ice the butter before mixing.

Wet by degrees, mixing and squeezing it lightly, forming first a crumby bread which, well worked by pressing the whole mass gradually between the wrists and the board, will incorporate the hard and soft parts.

For the pie:

Singe eight middle-sized snipe. Take off their necks and feet and cut them in two. Take out the backbone and after wiping the inside with a napkin, place them on a sauté plate in which you have melted butter, the same quantity of grated bacon (you scrape for this purpose bacon fat which produces a kind of lard), a tablespoon of parsley, two of mushrooms and four of truffles, all chopped very fine, then a small clove of shallot (blanched and chopped), a sufficient quantity of salt to season and some grated nutmeg.

Let them simmer on a moderate fire for 20 minutes, during which time take care to turn them, in order that they may be equally seasoned. This is called seasoning the snipe with sweet herbs.

Afterwards put them to cool and then chop the insides of the snipes and pound them in a mortar, adding to them four tablespoons of forcemeat, two of sweet herbs and some more nutmeg.

Line a seven-inch pie case with pastry and line this with the forcemeat, and after cutting out all the bony parts of the snipes to give them a handsome form, place them in the pie in the shape of a crown, adding between the snipes a few good truffles cut in slices which will communicate to them the flavour of the truffles, and then cover the whole with the seasoning mentioned before.

Two laurel leaves, with some round slices of larding bacon of the same size as the surface of the pie, are now placed upon it, which are covered afterwards with a piece of pastry.

Then pinch the rim, and ornament the whole, after which egg it well (an egg mixed with half a tablespoon of sifted flour will produce a beautiful effect in baking hot pies) and put it in a clear oven.

As soon as the top is lightly coloured, cut it off, and keep it, and cover the pie instead with four round pieces of paper nine inches in diameter.

Let it bake for an hour and half. Then take the cover off, the slices of bacon, and the laurel leaves, and after skimming off all the fat, mask the contents with chopped truffles and some glazed sauce Espagnol reduced by half. The crust is afterwards replaced and lightly glazed.

Be sure the pie be ready the moment you are going to serve it up, or it will lose part of its flavour.

CRÈME DE PIGEONNEAUX AUX MARRONS

Hôtel Talleyrand, 1815
Creamed squab with chestnuts

2 young pigeons
1 small hock of veal
2 tablespoons *mirepoix*
1 glass veal stock
2 pounds peeled chestnuts
1 head of celery
half a pint double cream
3 ounces unsalted butter
salt, pepper

Sweat in butter two pigeons and a small hock of veal with a *mirepoix*. Add a glass of bouillon and then two pounds of peeled chestnuts and a bunch of celery and cover and cook until all are soft.

Take out the pigeons, and remove the flesh, reserving the fillets for garnish. Pound the rest of the flesh and the chestnuts and press through a sieve.

Finish by adding cream and fresh butter and serve with the reserved fillets.

PETITS CROUSTADES DE CAILLES
Elysée Palace, 1815
Small bread croustades with quails

1 loaf stale French bread
6 quails
6 ounces clarified butter
half a pound forcemeat (see below)
12 rashers streaky bacon, unsmoked
sauce Espagnol (see above)

Take a stale French loaf and cut it into two-inch slices. Cut a hole in the middle of about two inches diameter. The same number of slices as quails. Fry these croustades in clarified butter and drain on a napkin.

Lay them on a baking tray and place first a spoonful of a good forcemeat and then a boned quail, chest upwards, into each.

Lay larded bacon over them, and paper. Let them bake in a moderate oven for an hour and half. Let them drain on a napkin, after which pour over them a good sauce Espagnol.

Instead of quails you may use larks or other small game. A claw may be retained to garnish each. Quails may similarly be baked all together in a croustade made from a large, fluted loaf from which the crumbs have been removed.

LES PETITS VOL-AU-VENTS À LA NESLE

Brighton Pavilion
and Château Rothschild

20 vol-au-vent cases, the diameter of a glass

20 cocks'-combs

20 cocks' stones (testes)

10 lambs' sweetbreads

(thymus and pancreatic glands, washed in water for five
   hours, until the liquid runs clear)

10 small truffles, pared, chopped, boiled in consommé

20 tiny mushrooms

20 lobster tails

4 fine whole lambs' brains, boiled and chopped

1 French loaf

2 spoonfuls chicken jelly

2 spoonful velouté sauce

1 tablespoon chopped parsley

2 tablespoons chopped mushrooms

4 egg yolks

2 chickens, boned

2 calves' udders

2 pints cream

sauce Allemande

salt, nutmeg

Forcemeat:

Crumb a whole French loaf. Add two spoonfuls of poultry jelly, one of velouté, one tablespoon of chopped parsley, two of mushrooms, chopped. Boil and stir as it thickens to a ball. Add two egg yolks. Pound the flesh of two boned chickens through a sieve. Boil two calves' udders – once cold, pound and pass through a sieve.

Then, mix six ounces of the breadcrumb *panada* to ten ounces of the chicken meat, and ten of the calves' udders and combine and pound for 15 minutes. Add five drams of salt, some nutmeg and the yolks of two more eggs and a spoonful of cold velouté or béchamel. Pound for a further ten minutes. Test by poaching a ball in boiling water – it should form soft, smooth balls.

Make some balls of poultry forcemeat in small coffee spoons, dip them in jelly broth and after draining on a napkin, place them regularly in the vol-au-vent, already half filled with:

a good ragout of cocks'-combs and stones (testicles)
lambs' sweetbreads (thymus and pancreatic glands,
    washed in water for five hours, until the liquid
    runs clear)
truffles
mushrooms
lobster tails
four fine whole brains.

Cover all with an extra thick sauce Allemande.

CAKES & PÂTISSERIE

—◦◦◦◦—

GÂTEAU PITHIVIER
(DE PITHIVIER according to Carême)
Carême's Pâtisserie, rue de la Paix, 1805

Pithiviers are now a staple of the pâtisserie. Carême lists many variations, but this is the classic. It can be made as one large 'cake' or as smaller petits fours.

8 ounces blanched almonds – crushed
6 ounces granulated sugar
2 ounces crushed macaroon biscuits (e.g. amaretti)
4 egg yolks
4 ounces butter
pinch of salt
4 tablespoons of whipped cream

Puff pastry – enough to roll out two circles of eight or nine inch diameter about an eighth of an inch thick (about a pound).

Roll out one round nine inches in diameter – with the trimmings, once a perfect circle has been cut, roll out another seven inches in diameter.

Lay the smaller circle on baking paper on a tray, and mound the almond and cream mixture into the middle, leaving an inch of pastry naked. Wet these edges with water, and lay the larger circle over and stick it down to the wet edges.

Egg-glaze the entire, and leave to cool for at least half an hour.

Then cut, with a very sharp knife, a sunflower or whirlwind pattern into the top (a star with curved rays), making sure not to cut all the way through the pastry. Notch around the edge with a knife or fork, and then make horizontal cuts in the pastry to help it rise at the edges.

Bake in a medium hot oven for about half an hour, until golden brown, then sift granulated sugar onto the top and return to the oven for five minutes.

Lemon Pithivier: as above with the zest of one lemon and an ounce of candied lemon peel in the stuffing.

GENOISES CAKES À LA MARASCHINO
Brighton Pavilion and Carlton House, 1817

Maraschino, the Prince Regent's favourite liqueur (it is said the prince downed 12 glasses before he could face his wedding night), was used repeatedly by Carême to flavour Brighton Pavilion recipes.

4 ounces almonds
half an egg white
2 whole eggs

Continued overleaf

6 ounces flour
6 ounces pounded sugar
6 ounces butter
zest of 1 orange
Maraschino brandy
salt
cochineal

Pound together four ounces of sweet almonds, half an egg white, and then add six ounces of flour and six ounces of pounded sugar.

Mix and add the zest of an orange, two whole eggs and a spoonful of Maraschino brandy, a grain of salt and splash of cochineal.

Stir this for a full six minutes with a spatula, then take six ounces of butter, softened in the mouth of an oven, stir it a little, and then put it in the corner of a tureen, mix it with a little of the paste, and then more, stirring the whole for four or five minutes longer.

Spread on a baking tray to the thickness of half an inch and level with a knife.

Put in a slack oven and as soon as the genoises are firm, cut them in all kinds of shapes, after which put them back in the oven to crisp.

LES FANCHONETTES AU CAFÉ MOCHA

Château Rothschild, 1829

A Carême favourite. For the modern palate, it is advised to halve the sugar.

6 ounces puff pastry
4 ounces Mocha coffee beans
3 glasses milk
4 egg yolks
5 egg whites
7 ounces castor sugar
1 ounce plain flour
salt
castor sugar for dusting

Roast four ounces of Mocha coffee over a moderate fire, shaking the pan continually, that the coffee may be regularly coloured. Once reddened, put into three glasses of boiling milk. Let stand for 15 minutes and then strain through a napkin.

In a small pan, place the yolks of four eggs and three ounces of pounded sugar, an ounce of sifted flour and a grain of salt. Mix together and add the Mocha infusion. Bring to boil on moderate fire, stirring continually with a spatula to prevent its sticking.

Make six ounces of puff pastry, turned 12 times, and rolled out to the thickness of one-sixth of an inch. Cover the inside of about 30 *mirlitons* (tartlet moulds) and pour a little of the cream into each. Bake till crusted and a golden brown. Leave to cool.

Fill remainder to near top. Smooth a thin layer of beaten egg white over the top (two egg whites beaten will do). Then decorate the top with small meringues (no larger than an almond) piped into a star pattern; seven round the outside, one in the middle. This meringue mixture to be made from the whites of three eggs, stiffly beaten and four ounces of pounded sugar. Dust all over the top with pounded sugar and bake, in a slack oven, till a fine reddish colour. Serve immediately.

MILANESE FLAN
Bailly's Pâtisserie, 1800

Carême's flans are entremets, which today would almost always be sweet, but for him were a side dish filling out the symmetrical pattern of service *à la française*. This is a little like a large, cheesy Yorkshire pudding.

8 ounces short crust pastry
2 quarts full cream milk
2 ounces butter
6 ounces rice flour
6 ounces unsalted butter
1 small Viry cheese
one and a half pounds grated Parmesan
8 eggs

4 egg yolks
6 egg whites
6 spoonfuls whipped cream
pepper
sugar

Put in a large stewpan a little more than two quarts of good milk, with two ounces of butter.

When boiling, work in as much rice flour as will make a paste of the thickness of *crème pâtissière* but somewhat firmer; reduce this cream for five minutes, and change it into another stewpan.

Mix with six ounces of fresh butter, a small Viry cheese and one and a half pounds of grated Parmesan cheese. Add four eggs, a pinch of mignonette pepper, twice as much pounded sugar, four more eggs and four yolks.

When mixed it should be the consistency of a soft pastry or a choux paste. Whip six egg whites very firm, and add them to the paste, with six spoonfuls of whipped cream. Put it in a croustade or pastry case and bake until it cracks golden like a brioche (more than two hours in a slow oven).

Serve on leaving the oven.

DESSERTS

—◦⦊⦉◦—

GELÉE D'ORANGES EN RUBANS
Château Rothschild, 1829
Oranges stuffed with orange and almond marbled jelly

The quantity of clarified sugar and isinglass varied according to the acidity of the fruit, and the closeness of the weather. (One sixth more isinglass in case of rain.)

12 oranges
juice of 2 lemons
cochineal
syrup to taste – 1 glass
1 pound French (sweet) almonds
20 bitter almonds
12 ounces sugar
water
isinglass or gelatine

Take one ounce, four drams of isinglass, cut into small pieces and wash in warm water.

Put on a fire in a middle-sized pan, with five glasses of filtered water, as soon as it boils, put in the corner of the stove such that it will continue boiling hard, taking care to skim it well.

As soon as it is reduced to three-fourths, strain it through a napkin into a clean vessel. Take a dozen oranges, and remove a 'plug' with a root cutter.

Reserve. Cut out the flesh with a coffee spoon, plunging the empty carcasses into cold water. If the orange rind breaks, plug immediately with a little butter. Place the empty hulks in crushed ice, two inches from each other.

Orange jelly:

Meanwhile strain the juice of the oranges through a bag, add the juice of two lemons, a little cochineal and cooled clarified syrup and the isinglass as above.

Blancmange:

After blanching one pound of sweet almonds and about 20 bitter almonds, throw them in cold water and wipe them. Pound with a clean mortar, moistening with water from a spoon, in order to prevent them turning into oil.

Dilute slowly with a silver spoon and filtered water and then squeeze them through a napkin to extract the almond milk.

Add to this 12 ounces of loaf sugar, pass again through a napkin and add an ounce of isinglass, a little more than lukewarm.*

Layer the orange jelly and blancmange in the oranges, leaving each layer to set (this can be tested by finger) – a spoonful at a time.

* gelatine can substitute.

When ready to serve, cut some in quarters with a very sharp knife to reveal the ribbons. Leave some intact, replugged, and arranged on napkins intermixed with green leaves.

FROMAGE BAVAROIS AUX NOIX VERTS
Brighton Pavilion, 1817
Bavarois cream with walnuts

Carême lists dozens of Bavarois – set creams. This one is not too complex, and the sweetness is to some extent modified by the walnuts.

25 walnuts
1 pint double cream
8 ounces sugar
isinglass or gelatine
1 pint whipped cream

Take 25 peeled walnuts – or count out 50 prepared walnut halves, and pound with one pint of cream and eight ounces of sugar. Leave to infuse for an hour, and then add the isinglass*
and set it to cool in the fridge for half an hour. When still not set, stir in a pint of thickly whipped cream. Set it immediately into a jelly mould or similar and leave overnight.

* gelatine can substitute.

᠄

SUÉDOIS DE PÊCHES
EN CROUSTADES
Salle de l'Opéra, Paris, 1804

Peaches, as served for Napoleon after his coronation at the dinner given by the Marshals of France. A croustade is a case – not necessarily meant to be eaten – made of pastry, puff pastry or bread and sometimes even semolina, rice or potato.

8-inch pie crust/croustade
18 peaches
water
8 ounces sugar
1 apple
1 tablespoon apricot jam
strawberries or grapes for garnish

Par-bake in a moderate oven a sweet, glazed pie crust, eight inches diameter. Arrange peach slices in the pie crust, to cover (about six peaches). Take 12 middling-sized peaches (nectarines can be used too) and fit them into a pan. Cover with water to only halfway up the peaches and add eight ounces of sugar. Bring to the boil and turn the peaches gently. The skins should begin to fall away from the peaches in the syrup. Remove them immediately into cold water, and remove the skins.

As the peaches are cooling, reduce the peach syrup by half. Add a chopped apple and some apricot jam to the syrup, and reduce further. Use half the syrup to pour over the peaches in the pie crust and bake another 15 minutes. Remove the core of the peaches whilst keeping it whole (cut in a circular motion from where the stalk once was) and push some of the cooled peach-apple marmalade syrup inside.

To arrange:

The pie will be slightly sticky and form the base of an impressive pyramid of stuffed baked peaches.

When cool, layer the peaches, seven on the lowest rank, then four, then one.

To garnish:

Use strawberries, or alternating black and white grape halves (Malaga and Muscadel). Or caramel can be drizzled over the pyramid – especially for apple suédois.

GELÉE DE VERJUS
The Tsar's marquee, Vertus, Champagne, 1815
Verjuice jelly

2 pounds sharp green grapes
1 handful spinach
1 pound sugar
isinglass or gelatine
Madeira – enough to cover and poach fruit

Take two pounds of fine green (sour or wine) grapes pounded with a handful of fresh spinach. When well beaten, run the juice though a bag of muslin, which should yield a clear liquid of a light green colour. Mix with one pound of clarified sugar, one and half ounces of isinglass. Set around fruits cooked in Madeira.

For the modern cook: gelatine again can substitute. It is difficult to buy grapes-from-the-vine, as opposed to sweet table grapes. Lessen the sugar as appropriate. If setting around fruit poached in Madeira (pears work well), simply add sugar to taste.

෴

PUDDING À LA NESSELRODE
Hôtel Talleyrand, 1815
Nesselrode pudding

In 1814 Count von Nesselrode entered Paris with the Russians, and camped under the chestnut trees of the Champs-Elysée. Talleyrand sent word to Nesselrode and the Tsar that the Elysée Palace was undermined, and the Tsar agreed to stay with Talleyrand until the palace was safe. Carême may have been the messenger. In any event, he created a chestnut pudding in honour of the Russian minister with the German name that became a favourite of a British king, George IV.

40 chestnuts

water

1 pound sugar

1 stick vanilla

1 pint double cream

12 egg yolks

3 egg whites

1 glass Maraschino brandy

1 plateful whipped cream

1 ounce candied lemon peel, 2 ounces currants, 2 ounces
    raisins, all soaked overnight in Maraschino brandy

Take 40 chestnuts and blanch in boiling water, pound them
and add a few spoonfuls of syrup, and then press through a
sieve. Mix with a pint of syrup made from one pound of sugar
clarified with a stick of vanilla, and place in a bowl with a pint
of double cream and 12 fresh egg yolks.

Set this over a gentle heat, and, stirring constantly, take
it off just as it is about to boil. Pass through a sieve again.
Once cold, add a glass of Maraschino brandy. (Let it set on
ice overnight.)

Then add an ounce of candied lemon peel, two ounces of
currants and two ounces of raisins that have all been soaked
overnight in Maraschino. Mix and add another 'plateful' of
whipped cream, and three egg whites, stiffly beaten.

Mould it in a pewter mould, the shape of a pineapple, so
that the pudding receives the form of a dome imitating a pineapple. The mould should close like those used by confectioners

for iced creams; when thus moulded, place it again in the freezing pan covered with ice and saltpetre.

*The recipe will work in an ice-cream maker, or the whole can be semi-frozen, but then the last 'plateful' of cream added before the whole is set in a mould overnight in the fridge. To the modern palate this is extremely sweet. The substitution of lemon peel for candied lemon peel, and the omission of some of the raisins might not have pleased the Prince Regent but did please recent dinner guests. Maraschino is quite difficult to come by – cherry brandy or the syrup from cocktail cherries is not a bad substitute.

MERINGUES DES POMMES
EN HERRISON
Brighton Pavilion, 1817
Apple meringue as a hedgehog

40 apples
6 ounces sugar
peel of 1 lemon
half a jar apricot jam
2 egg whites
2 tablespoons icing sugar
castor and granulated sugar to dust
8 ounces sliced almonds
4 ounces sliced pistachios

After coring forty apples with an apple scoop, peel 15 of them quite round, putting each apple, as soon as it is peeled, in water, in the same way as for a suédois. Take eight and boil them in six ounces of clarified sugar, taking care that they remain a little firm.

In the meantime peel the remaining seven and put them to boil immediately after taking the first out of the syrup. Remove when still firm. The remaining 25 should be peeled and cut in slices and added to the syrup with the peel of a lemon, and the whole put on a moderate fire.

When the apples are dissolved, stir them till they are reduced to a perfect marmalade, and rub them through a sieve, and then add half a pot of apricot marmalade. When cold, spread two spoonfuls of this apple/apricot marmalade on an oven-proof serving dish on which you then place nine of the largest whole apples, on them five more, and the last on top.

First put some marmalade on the inside of the apples, and fill up the vacancies with more. With the remainder of the marmalade, cover the entire in such a manner that the whole forms a perfect dome.

Then beat the whites of two eggs very stiff, and add to it two spoonfuls of fine sugar. Spread this meringue over the apples as regularly as possible, and then cover it all with fine sugar.

Take some sweet almonds, sliced all exactly the same and stick them lightly but evenly on the sugar a quarter of an inch apart. When you have finished, strew some more coarse sugar over the whole, and place your dish in a slack oven, in order that the almonds as well as the egg and sugar may become light coloured. You may afterwards add some pistachios each cut in six fillets, placing them in small holes made with a silver skewer. Your dish is then put back in the oven for ten minutes and placed on the table as soon as you take it out.

SELECT BIBLIOGRAPHY

Works by Carême:

Le Pâtissier royal parisien, ou Traité élémentaire et pratique de la pâtisserie ancienne et moderne, suivi d'observations utiles au progrès de cet art, et d'une revue critique des grands bals de 1810 et 1811, Marie Antoine Carême (Paris, 1815)

Le Maître d'hôtel français, ou Parallèle de la cuisine ancienne et moderne, considérée sous le rapport de l'ordonnance des menus selon les quatre saisons, Marie Antoine Carême (Paris, 1822)

Le Cuisinier parisien, Deuxième édition, revue, corrigée et augmentée, Marie Antoine Carême (Paris, 1828)

L'Art de la cuisine française au dix-neuvième siècle. Traité élémentaire et pratique, (Volumes 1–5, Continued by A. Plumerey. The whole edited by C. F. A. Fayot), Marie Antoine Carême (Paris, 1833–1847)

Le Pâtissier pittoresque, précédé d'un traité des cinq ordres d'architecture, Marie Antoine Carême (4ème edition, Paris, 1842)

Projets d'architecture pour l'embellissement de Sainte Petersbourg, Marie Antoine Carême (Paris, 1821)

Projets d'architecture pour l'embellissement de Paris, Marie Antoine Carême (Paris, 1826)

The royal Parisian pastrycook and confectioner, From the original of M.A. Carême, ed. John Porter, Marie Antoine Carême (F.J. Mason, 1834)

French Cookery, Comprising L'Art de la cuisine française; Le Pâtissier royal; Le Cuisinier parisien... translated by William Hall, Marie Antoine Carême (John Murray, London, 1836)

Antonin Carême 1783–1833, La Sensualité gourmande en Europe, Georges Bernier (Grasset, Paris, 1989)

Antonin Carême de Paris, 1783–1833, Louis Rodil (Editions Jeanne Laffitte, Marseille, 1980)

L'Art culinaire au XIXè siècle, Antonin Carême 1784–1984, Catalogue de l'exposition tenue à la Mairie du IIIè arrondissement (La Mairie de Paris, Paris, 1984)

Les Classiques de la table, (Mémoires et Souvenirs inédits d'Antonin Carême), Marquis de Cussy (Paris, 1843)

——————

L'alimentation et la technique culinaire à travers les siècles, étude suivie de La Vie professionnelle de Carême, Philéas Gilbert (Paris, 1928)

Petit Bréviaire de la gourmandise, Laurent Tailhade (Albert Messein, Paris, 1919)

La Vie privée d'autrefois, Alfred Franklin (Paris, 1888)

La Physiologie du goût, Jean-Anthelme Brillat-Savarin, ed. Jean François Revel (Fammarion, Paris, 1982)

Brillat-Savarin: The Judge and his Stomach, Giles MacDonogh (John Murray, London, 1992)

A Palate in Revolution, Grimod de la Reynière and the Almanach des Gourmands, Giles MacDonogh (Robin Clark, 1987)

Dr William Kitchener, Author of The Cook's Oracle, Tom Bridge and Colin Cooper English (Southover Press, 1992)

A History of Cooks and Cooking, Michael Symons (Prospect Books, 2001)

The Invention of the Restaurant, Rebecca L. Spang (Harvard University Press, 2000)

Feast, A History of Grand Eating, Roy Strong (Jonathan Cape, 2002)

Consuming Passions, A History of English Food and Appetite, Philippa Pullar (Penguin, 2001)

Food, A History, Felipe Fernandez-Armesto (Macmillan, 2001)

Le Repertoire de la Cuisine, Louis Saulmier, trans. E. Brunet (Leon Jaeggi & Sons, 1982)

British Cutlery, ed. Peter Brown (York Civic Trust, Philip Wilson, 2001)

Great Cooks and their Recipes from Taillevent to Escoffier, Anne Willan (Pavilion, 2000)

Larousse Gastronomique (Hamlyn, 2001)

Lady Morgan in France, ed. Elizabeth Suddaby and P. J. Yarrow (Oriel Press, 1971)

Lady Morgan: The Life and Times of Sydney Owenson, Mary Campbell (Pandora, 1988)

Une Irlandaise Libérale en France sous la restauration: Lady Morgan, 1775–1859, Marcel Ian Moraud (Paris, 1954)

Talleyrand, Duff Cooper (Jonathan Cape, 1932)

Talleyrand, ou Le cynisme, André Castelot (Paris, 1980)

La duchesse de Dino, princesse de Courlande, égérie de Talleyrand, 1793–1862, Micheline Dupuy (Paris, 2002)

Napoleon, Vincent Cronin (Collins, 1971)

Napoleon and Josephine: An Improbable Marriage, Evangeline Bruce (Weidenfeld and Nicolson, 1995)

Napoleon & Marie Louise, Alan Palmer (Constable, 2001)

Marie Antoinette, Antonia Fraser (Weidenfeld and Nicolson, 2001)

Madame de la Tour du Pin, Memoirs: Laughing and Dancing Our Way to the Precipice, trans. Felice Harcourt (Harvill, 1969)

France 1789–1815: Revolution and Counterrevolution, D.M.G. Sutherland (Collins, 1985)

French Society in Revolution 1789–1799, David Andress (Manchester University Press, 1999)

The French Wars 1792–1815, Charles J. Esdaile (Routledge, 2001)

-◄◄◄◆►►►-

1815: The Roads to Waterloo, Gregor Dallas (Richard Cohen Books, 1996)

George IV: The Grand Entertainment, Steven Parissien (John Murray, 2001)

George IV, Christopher Hibbert (Harmondsworth, 1976)

Prince of Pleasure, Saul David (Little, Brown, 1998)

The Royal Pavilion Brighton, John Dinkel (Philip Wilson, 1983)

The Royal Interiors of Regency England, David Watkin (Dent, 1984)

The Making of the Brighton Pavilion, John Morley (Philip Wilson, 1984)

The Royal Pavilion, Brighton, Jessica Rutherford (Brighton Borough Council, 1995)

The Disastrous Marriage, Joanna Richardson (Jonathan Cape, 1960)

High Society: A Social History of the Regency 1788–1830, Venetia Murray (Viking, 1998)

-‹‹‹•›››-

Alexander I: Tsar of War and Peace, Alan Palmer (Weidenfeld & Nicolson, 1974)

Natasha's Dance, A Cultural History of Russia, Orlando Figes (Allen Lane, 2002)

Pavlovsk: The Life of a Russian Palace, Suzanne Massie (Little, Brown, 1990)

Russia and the Russians, Geoffrey Hosking (Allen Lane, 2001)

Napoleon in Russia, Alan Palmer (André Deutsch, 1967)

St Petersburg, A Cultural History, Solomon Volkov, trans. Antonina W. Bouis (Free Press, 1995)

The Hermitage: The Biography of a Great Museum, Geraldine Norman (Jonathan Cape, 1997)

-‹‹‹•›››-

Lives of Lord Castlereagh and Sir Charles Stewart, the second and third Marquesses of Londonderry. With annals of contemporary events in which they bore a part. From the original papers of the family, Sir Archibald Alison (Blackwood & Sons: Edinburgh and London, 1861)

Castlereagh, C.J. Bartlett (Macmillan 1966)

Frances Anne: The Life and Times of Frances Anne, Marchioness of Londonderry, and Her Husband Charles, Third Marquess of Londonderry, Edith Helen Vane Tempest, Marchioness of Londonderry (Macmillan & Co, London, 1958)

⠀⠀⠀⠀⠀⠀⠀⠀⠀⠀⠀⠀⠀⠀⠀⠀●

Baron James and the Rise of the French Rothschilds, Anka Muhlstein (Collins, 1983)

James de Rothschild: 1792–1868, Une métamorphose, une légende, Anka Muhlstein (Gallimard, Paris, 1981)

The Rothschilds: A European Family, edited by Georg Heuberger published on behalf of the Frankfurt Municipal Office for Culture and Leisure for the Exhibition 'The Rothschilds a European Family' in the Frankfurt Museum of the City of Frankfurt-am-Main 11 October 1994–27 February 1995 (Thorbecke/Boydell and Brewer 1994)

Les Rothschilds Batisseurs et mécènes, Pauline Prevost-Marcilhacy (Flammarion, Paris 1995)

Paris Between the Empires: 1814–1852, Philip Mansel (John Murray, 2001)

ACKNOWLEDGEMENTS (2003)

Firstly, Kate Chisholm, to whom I owe thanks beyond measure for all her encouragement, judicious advice and tactful editing, and for introducing me in the first place to Short Books and, via Fanny Burney, to Antonin Carême. I must immediately acknowledge my debt to the research of Georges Berniers and Louis Rodil on the life and career of Carême – without their recipes to follow this book would have taken many more years to write.

The insights of Rebecca Spang, Orlando Figes, Alan Palmer and Anka Muhlstein have similarly proved invaluable in understanding the many worlds Carême inhabited. But this book could not have been written at all without the generous encouragement of my parents, brothers and friends – and the forbearance of the casts and crews of the various other projects that have punctuated my writing: the Russian-Chechen film, *Voina,* and the plays *Relative Values* and *A Busy Day* – to all, many thanks.

I am also greatly indebted to the chefs Eric and Hülya Rousseau at Belle Epoque Pâtisserie, London – for helping me recreate various Carême recipes, and for insisting I actually plunge my hand into boiling sugar – and to Mark

Dodson at Cliveden Hotel, Buckinghamshire, Tom Illic at the Threadneedles Hotel, London, the staff at Pâtisserie Valerie, Soho, and to the wonderful cook, Pat Kelly, my mother – all of whom have allowed me to invade their kitchens for the purposes of this book.

For their hospitality during the travels involved in writing this book, I would like to thank Brendan and Coralie Hooper, Sinead Cusack and Jeremy Irons, Sir John Lyons, Mo and Tim Guthrie-Harrison, Sara Crowe and Sean Carson, and Neil and Ann Hodgkiss.

For their inspired comments and suggestions on the text I am forever grateful to my dear friends Erica Wagner, Sasha Damianovsky, Victoria Kortes-Papp, my stalwart literary agent Anthony Harwood, and of course the excellent Aurea Carpenter at Short Books. Thanks, too, to Georgia Vaux for her talent and keen eye.

In France

For her help as *châtelaine*, *chef de cuisine* and in correcting my French, Lady Danielle Lyons; also Serge Gatinel, Madame Vany, Florence Tison, Marc du Pouget and Monique Carrilou at Château Valençay, and all the staff at the Bibliotèque Nationale. My sincere thanks are due as well to the Societé des Cuisiniers in Paris for their assistance, and to Jeremy Close, Simon Packard, L'Hôtel on rue des Beaux Arts and the Park Hyatt Paris-Vendôme, rue de la Paix, and also Anne Cooke-Yarborough and Matthias Fournier.

In St Petersburg

Special thanks must go to Tobin Auber – for his diligence on behalf of the Carême project, but also his translation (actual and cultural) of all things Russian, and for his wise counsel and friendship – and also to Alexei Balabanov, Alexei Chadov, Olga Chernyshova, Simon Sebag-Montefiore and Dr Sergei Kuznetsov at the Stroganoff Palace; and to Kenny McInnes, Anastasia Mikliaeva at the State Hermitage Museum, and A Gusanov and Nikolai Sergeivich Tretiakov at the State Pavlovsk Palace Museum, and to Yulia and Demi for taking me there. And in memory of Sergei Bodrov Jr.

In London and Brighton

Melanie Aspey and Laura Schor at the Rothschild Archive, the Marquess of Londonderry, Lady Mary and the staff at Mount Stewart, Jessica Rutherford and Shirley Lobo at the Brighton Pavilion and the staff of the Public Records Office in Kew, the Royal Archive in Windsor and the British Library. For help with the diagnosis of Carême's final illness I am indebted to the Wellcome Institute and to my brother Andrew Kelly, FRCS Orth.

Deserving thanks that can only be repaid by my love are Mum and Dad, who inspired me with a love of food in the first place, and Claire, who bore, during the course of my writing this, not only with my imaginative and actual absences whilst exploring Carême's world and with all my attempts – more and less successful – at 18th-century recipes, but who also, latterly, bore our son, Oscar.

ACKNOWLEDGEMENTS (2025)

Thanks, twenty-one years later:

For the progress of the book and play and now TV series, but in no particular, order thanks to: Simon Green, Peter Tear, Maya Baran, George Gibson, Elizabeth Kleinhans, Ellen and Arthur Wagner, Joe Harmston, Martha Teichner, Florence Fabricant, the staff of the French Laundry, and chefs Tom Illic, Heston Blumenthal, Jean Christophe Novelli, Michel Roux, Mark Meltonville and Richard Fitch, and the irrepressible Ivan Day.

Amanda Ross and all on the then-*Richard & Judy Show*, The Ideas Foundry, Ryan Early, George Taylor, Tom Rand, Joanna Morgan and all at 59E59 Theaters, New York, and for the actual premiere of *Cooking for Kings*, the play: the Strangford Lough Food Festival and Ballywalter Park Newtonards and Brian and Vibse, Lord and Lady Dunleath and Deborah Shaw then of Bath Theatre Royal Productions.

For this edition, my special thanks to Paul Baggaley, Gurdip Ahluwalia, Faye Robinson and all at Bloomsbury, London and New York. Special thanks to those who encouraged and guided me on the journey towards a TV adaptation, especially Taylor Downing and all at Flashback Productions and the team at the

Royal Pavilion, Brighton. Annie and Richard LaGravenese, Julian Fellowes, Craig Turk, Judith Regan, Lauren Goldstein-Crowe Gub Neal, David Flynn, Atlas Productions, Los Angeles, Tom Stoppard and Simon Russell Beale, and for the journey specifically towards Vanessa van Zuylen in Paris, and on to AppleTV: Louise Chater, Nick Manzi, Cathy King, and in LA, Sarah Arnott, Eric Williams and the team at Zero Gravity Management, and Will Jacobson and Demien Tirsch, and then in Paris, via Elizabeth Segerstrom, Andrew von Oeyen, Stephen Geerts and Melissa Lesnie to Siv Huor, of Yungo Law, Beatrice Pacotte, and in London, Jonathan Davies-Jones KC. Vanessa van Zuylen is a visionary and I will always think of her as a friend. At one point she more or less saved my life. She also took my teenage daughter aside and told her 'what every Frenchwoman knows'. (No: they won't tell me.)

I should give special mention and thanks to David Edgar, whom I first met filming 'Regency Banquet' at the Brighton Pavilion but whose faith and friendship over the years, and confidence in the idea of Carême on screen sustained me perhaps more than anyone. And to my family, again, who soon tired of Carême recreations but are carriers of a different sort of flame. Oscar's fantasy cakes were and are a thing of wonder, as is he, as is Celia.

A Note on the Author

Ian Kelly is an actor and writer. He has lived and worked in France, Russia, South America and the United States, and writes frequently about food and travel for many British publications, including *The Times* and the *Guardian*.